LIVING
WITH
SCHIZOPHRENIA

An Holistic Approach to
Understanding, Preventing and Recovering
from "Negative" Symptoms

by

John Watkins

9

First published in Australia 1996
by Hill of Content Publishing Company Pty Ltd
86 Bourke Street, Melbourne, Australia 3000
Reprinted 1998

© John Watkins 1996

Cover design: Deborah Snibson, The Modern Art Production Group
Typeset by: Figment, Fitzroy, Melbourne
Printed in Australia by: The Australian Print Group, Maryborough

National Library of Australia cataloguing-in-publication data

Watkins, John, 1951–
    Living with schizophrenia: an holistic approach to understanding, preventing
    and recovering from negative symptoms.

    Bibliography.
    Includes index.
    ISBN 0 85572 272 X.

    1. Schizophrenia. 2. Schizophrenics – Rehabilitation. I. Title.

616.8982

The time has come to go beyond the categorisations,
the old images, and the destructive expectations.
Our hope lies in hope: creating a climate of
support, learning, and encouragement
for those who seem to have
no reason left
for hope.

– *Marcia Lovejoy*

For those of us who have been diagnosed with
mental illness, hope is not just a nice
sounding euphemism. It is a
matter of life and
death.

– *Patricia Deegan*

Thus there can be no doubt at all that the
psyche's capacity to produce affects
has not disappeared in
schizophrenia.

– *Eugen Bleuler*

NOTE TO READERS

This book is intended for both lay and professional readers. It is the sincere hope of the author that *anyone* who is interested in trying to understand and work more creatively with problems related to schizophrenia, and in particular with the so-called "negative" symptoms, will find much of value herein.

In order to enhance "reader-friendliness" every effort has been made to minimise the use of complicated psychiatric terminology and jargon. At the same time, however, professional readers will find that extensive reference has been made to the technical literature in order to support the arguments made and to facilitate further research into this much neglected area. (Numbers throughout the text refer to notes which begin on page 118.)

Readers who are primarily interested in preventing or alleviating "negative" symptoms will find many *practical strategies* simply and clearly described in Part Two.

CONTENTS

CONTENTS (continued)

PREFACE

This book is the product of more than twenty years of experience and reflection. When I first started to put these ideas down on paper some fifteen years ago I wanted to show that much of the apparently unexplainable or even frankly "bizarre" behaviour of people who receive a diagnosis of schizophrenia actually has a meaning and a purpose if only we can see it. My own clinical experience as a psychiatric nurse had shown me this quite clearly. I have discovered, however, that not everyone does see this. In fact, some people seem to be quite hostile to the very suggestion, as if it somehow challenged a view of things that they did not want to change. Sadly, it seems that this reluctance has become even stronger in some quarters over the past decade or two. There are undoubtedly many complex reasons for this, though a full discussion of them goes well beyond the scope of this book.

In the meanwhile it is sufficient to acknowledge that there are a number of powerful forces at work which seem to make it difficult for us to remain in touch with the fact that whatever else it may involve, schizophrenia is first and foremost about people. Suffering people, troubled people – sometimes even *troubling* people – but people nonetheless! Examples of the tendency to forget this truth are easy to find. For example, many of the textbooks which are used by mental health professionals contain chapters with titles such as "The Treatment of Schizophrenia" or "The Rehabilitation of Schizophrenia". These chapters and the information they contain may be studied and discussed at great length without anyone ever realising that it makes no sense to talk about treating "schizophrenia" as if it were something that had a real and tangible existence of its own. After all, it is surely only possible to treat a *person* who has a diagnosis of schizophrenia? Or to rehabilitate a *person* who has lost their way in life and needs help in re-acquiring the skills and confidence to begin finding it again? Viewing "schizophrenia" as if it were something that exists in the brain independently of the affected person makes as much sense as trying to understand the behaviour and motives of the various characters in a television programme by looking in the back of the TV set!

Many people in the mental health field now experience – and some freely admit – a growing unease with the extent to which purely biological explanations for human suffering have overtaken the person-centred approaches of earlier times. Of course biology *is* important, and the study of the various biological aspects of schizophrenia ought to be continued. It is increasingly clear, however, that human beings are multi-faceted organisms in which *every* part – biological, psychological, social, spiritual – is connected in a highly intricate and inter-dependent fashion with every other part. For this reason no individual facet can be properly understood in isolation from any other. This understanding, which is sometimes referred to as the *holistic* perspective, has contributed a great deal to our understanding and treatment of many forms of physical illness. Such an holistic perspective is well overdue in the mental health field. I sincerely hope that *Living With Schizophrenia* will help the process of bringing it into existence.

My sincerest thanks go to Fiona Smith, Bill Healy, Hans Stampfer, David Leach, and Michelle Anderson. I especially value the inspiring example that Patricia Deegan has provided through her writing and personal wisdom. I have gained much both professionally and personally from my contact with many people who have struggled to find a way of living with schizophrenia. I owe special thanks to Andrew, Michael and Pat who have willingly allowed me to use them as sounding boards, and to all those whose wonderfully unique way of being in this world has challenged me to keep thinking even when I thought I already knew all the answers.

John Watkins

Part One

Understanding "Negative" Symptoms

INTRODUCTION

Anyone who has close personal involvement with schizophrenia, either through their own experience or as a helper or carer, very soon discovers that in the long run it is often not the so-called "positive" symptoms such as delusions and hallucinations which are the most distressing and challenging, but rather those patterns of behaviour now commonly referred to as "negative" symptoms. Thus, for many people, problems related to such "negative" symptoms as reduced emotional expressiveness, lack of motivation, and social withdrawal are a major and on-going cause of frustration, despair, and – eventually – loss of hope.

Sadly, very little real help has usually been made available to people struggling with these problems. Prominent among the many reasons for this has been the fact that our understanding of the nature and causes of "negative" symptoms has for a long time been extremely limited. Historically, "negative" symptoms have usually been thought of as being amongst the core or intrinsic symptoms of schizophrenia. In recent years, as most psychiatric research has concentrated on attempts to discover possible biological "causes" of schizophrenia, it has often been assumed that every aspect of this disorder must have a biological basis. From this assumption has grown the expectation that if effective therapy for "negative" symptoms is to be developed, it will necessarily come in the form of some type of *physical* treatment (for example, new types of medication).

Whilst awaiting the promised fruits of the on-going biological research into schizophrenia many people are left feeling helpless and hopeless, yet still with a real desire to find some way of assisting those whose lives seem doomed to remaining forever "stuck" in apathy and despair. Their unanswered questions arise again and again: Are these problems *only* biological? Is there *really* nothing that can be done?

In his struggles with similar questions the renowned neurologist Dr. Oliver Sacks concluded that useful answers can often be found by replacing the usual disease-centred approach with a *person-centred* one. Though he treated patients with definite physical dysfunction of their central nervous systems, Dr. Sacks realised that many of the "symptoms" he observed were in fact the reactions and responses of people as they attempted to cope with and adapt to their difficult situations in the best way they were able. Eventually, as he came to see that no person is ever simply a passive victim of whatever may be malfunctioning in their brain, Dr. Sacks insisted that:

> It must be said from the outset that a disease is never a mere loss or excess – that there is always a reaction, on the part of the affected organism or individual, to restore, to replace, to compensate for and to preserve its identity, however strange the means may be: and to study or influence these means, no less than the primary insult to the nervous system, is an essential part of our role as physicians.[1]

Adopting a person-centred approach to schizophrenia helps to illuminate many aspects of this mysterious condition. Indeed, from this point of view even delusions and hallucinations might be seen as the affected person's attempts to cope with their extremely difficult circumstances. Interestingly, this was the belief of Professor Eugen Bleuler, the renowned Swiss psychiatrist who introduced the term "schizophrenia" to psychiatry in 1911.

An holistic, person-centred approach to "negative" symptoms reveals that there are many extremely important aspects of these problems that are very often overlooked. Furthermore, adopting such an approach makes it possible to integrate a range of observations from recent research to develop a new and more hopeful understanding of why and how these behaviours occur, and a greater appreciation of some of the many factors which may contribute to causing them. Even more importantly, *an holistic approach helps to clarify some of the many practical strategies which may help in preventing or alleviating these extremely common problems.*

In line with these views, many researchers now agree that:

- *"Negative" symptoms are not unique to schizophrenia.*
  Similar patterns of behaviour are often observed, for example, in depressed people, in neglected residents of custodial institutions (e.g. prisons, nursing and old age homes), and amongst the long-term unemployed.

- *"Negative" symptoms may have many causes.*
  Even when they occur in people who have a diagnosis of schizophrenia, "negative" symptoms may have many causes, not all of which are directly related to schizophrenia itself.

- *"Negative" symptoms can often be prevented or alleviated.*
  Rather than being an intrinsic aspect of schizophrenia which is permanent and essentially untreatable, many "negative" symptoms are related to potentially treatable (and sometimes even preventable) causes.

These views are consistent with the opinions expressed by many prominent internationally regarded authorities on schizophrenia. Many of these experts now believe that a distinction must be made between *primary* "negative" symptoms, which are thought to possibly be an intrinsic part of the schizophrenic disturbance, and *secondary* "negative" symptoms, which are related to psychological defence mechanisms and the social and emotional reactions of the diagnosed person. This distinction has enormous implications. Whilst the exact nature and origin of primary "negative" symptoms remains enigmatic, many secondary "negative" symptoms seem likely to be related to a range of identifiable and potentially treatable psychological, social and spiritual causes.

Since these symptoms may be outwardly identical it is usually impossible to tell simply by examination if a particular person has primary "negative" symptoms, secondary "negative" symptoms, or possibly a mixture of both. Leading researchers have therefore strongly emphasised the importance of avoiding any premature assumption that all "negative" symptoms occurring in a person with a diagnosis of schizophrenia are essentially untreatable when many may, in fact, be treatable secondary "negative" symptoms. *Failing to make this distinction and ascribing all withdrawal or apathy to unproven biological causes runs the tragic risk of giving up on some people and thus condemning them to a hopeless and limited existence quite unnecessarily.*

A more rational and compassionate approach would involve attempting to identify and modify as many as possible of the factors which may be contributing to the person's difficulties. Any "negative" symptoms which remain after a thorough and intensive effort of this kind has been made might then be assumed to be of the primary kind. (Even then, however, it may be unwise to assume these symptoms are permanent and untreatable since even so-called primary "negative" symptoms sometimes appear to fluctuate over time.)

In **Part One** of this book a number of the possible psychological, emotional and social causes of "negative" symptoms are discussed. The role of neuroleptic medication, the connection between brain functioning and "negative" symptoms, and the long-term outlook for people with these problems are also examined. Whilst many of the views expressed in this section are based upon "objective" scientific research, extensive use has also been made of "subjective" sources of information – including the first hand reports of people who have themselves experienced "negative" symptoms. These often touching personal testimonies have richly enhanced what scientific research has revealed, thereby helping to provide a unique perspective which emphasises the particularly *human* nature of these problems.

After reading this section some readers may find themselves wondering whether patterns of behaviour which include *coping mechanisms* such as withdrawal and "shut-down" should be referred to as "negative" symptoms. These readers may be reassured to know that they are in good company. Professor John Strauss, who along with some of his colleagues first used the term "negative" symptoms in regard to schizophrenia in 1974, has recently said that this term can be misleading since it does not adequately reflect the fact that some of these symptoms may represent *active coping* on the part of the patient.[2] In other words, rather than being "symptoms the person has got", some of these behaviours are actually "coping strategies the person is using". It is important to note that active coping strategies usually only account for *part* of the "negative" symptom picture, however, and that other factors (such as demoralisation or medication side-effects) are often also important. (Despite its obvious limitations the term "negative" symptoms has been used throughout this book simply because it is now widely used and, at the time of writing, appears to be growing in popularity.)

In **Part Two** a range of practical strategies are described which may help in preventing or alleviating *secondary* "negative" symptoms. (Many of these practical strategies may also help with other problems related to schizophrenia.) Whilst no guarantees can be given regarding their effectiveness in any particular case, all of the suggestions deserve careful consideration. Because of the complex and highly individual nature of the problems being addressed, only a "try-it-and-see" approach will reveal whether or not any of the specific strategies may prove to be helpful.

Whatever effect any of the strategies may or may not have, it is nevertheless sincerely hoped that at the very least this book will help to provide readers with the knowledge and confidence to think about "negative" symptoms in a new way. **This in itself might herald the beginnings of a significant change for the better!**

WHAT ARE THE "NEGATIVE" SYMPTOMS OF SCHIZOPHRENIA?

According to the American Psychiatric Association,[3] schizophrenia usually involves a number of so-called "negative" symptoms which can occur in addition to "positive" (psychotic) symptoms such as delusions and hallucinations. Typical "negative" symptoms can include the following:

- *Decreased range and intensity of emotional responsiveness.* This is technically referred to as "blunting" or "flattening" of affect and involves a significant reduction in the person's facial and vocal expression of emotions.

- *Poverty of thought* ("alogia"). This involves an apparent impoverishment of the person's thought processes. It is inferred from a noticeable reduction in the amount of spontaneous speech, brief and concrete replies to questions, or speech which seems to convey very little information.

- *Loss of motivation or drive* ("avolition"). This is reflected in the person's reduced ability to initiate or persist in goal-directed activities, and their apparent lack of interest in participating in work or social activities.

- *Diminished capacity to experience pleasure* ("anhedonia"). This is manifested as a reduction in the person's ability to enjoy recreational interests and activities, intimate friendships, or sex.

- *Social isolation and withdrawal.* The person tends to become uncommunicative and may show a marked preference for being alone. Some people may even actively avoid social situations.

Some or all of these "negative" symptoms may be present during, or following, a psychotic episode. Sometimes, a person may develop prominent "negative" symptoms *before* they have actually ever experienced a psychotic episode.´

As with every other aspect of schizophrenia, individual variations are the rule. Thus, there are some people who never seem to experience significant "negative" symptoms at all, whilst others may have only very mild or transient problems of this kind. There are those, however, for whom "negative" symptoms are both severe and prolonged. Such persons tend to be apathetic and lacking in drive. They appear to be slowed down both physically and mentally, and show a marked lack of spontaneity in their thinking and speech. Their reduced capacity for emotional responsiveness may cause them to feel "empty" or "hollow" inside and may, in extreme cases, give them a "wooden" or even "robot-like" appearance. They generally show little interest in initiating contact with others and may even actively avoid it by means of social withdrawal. People who are severely affected in this way may begin to drift further and further away from human contact, until eventually they come to live in a cocoon of ever deepening isolation.

"Negative" symptoms may persist for quite a long time after a psychotic episode has ended. Unlike "positive" symptoms, they often respond little – if at all – to the neuroleptic drugs which are the usual medical treatment for schizophrenia. In fact, these drugs may sometimes contribute to a worsening of problems such as slowness and lack of motivation. Consequently, serious difficulties and frustrations arise both for the affected person and for those who are involved with him or her. All too often it seems that there is very little that anyone can do to help. The affected person may even be told that the best thing they can do is to learn to adjust to a permanently lowered level of functioning for the rest of their life.

Any person who continues to feel lifeless, cut-off, and apathetic may inevitably begin to wonder if they will ever again experience joy or satisfaction, and even if life – such as it is – is really worth living. Family members, friends, and other helpers are also prone to despair. After a period (possibly a very long one) of attempting to push, or encourage, or even cajole a person out of their apathetic state, these efforts may gradually begin to taper off as physical and emotional exhaustion take their toll. Feelings of resignation may begin to grow until eventually – perhaps even with some sense of relief – inertia may appear to triumph as everyone begins to give up and accept what seems to be inevitable. Thus may begin the kind of "twilight" existence that many people have learnt to think of as the tragically inevitable and essentially unchangeable end-state commonly referred to as "chronic" schizophrenia.

WHAT CAUSES "NEGATIVE" SYMPTOMS?

As with schizophrenia itself, no one fully understands just why "negative" symptoms occur. In recent years, as biological theories in psychiatry have grown in popularity, one very commonly held view is that schizophrenic symptoms are related to physical changes in the brain. According to this view, "positive" symptoms such as delusions and hallucinations are often said to be linked to specific changes in the brain's biochemical functioning (e.g. to a "chemical imbalance"). "Negative" symptoms, on the other hand, are said to possibly be associated with certain changes in the actual physical *structure* of the brain.[4]

Whatever the possible roles of brain functioning, biochemistry and genes may prove to be in the causation of schizophrenia, a sensitive understanding of the **whole** person demands that adequate attention must also be given to the influence of *non-physical factors*.[5] Indeed, there is very good reason to believe that psychological, social and spiritual factors – which are bound to play a significant part in *every* facet of human behaviour – may be especially important in regard to the development and persistence of many of the "negative" symptoms of schizophrenia. In line with this view, Professor John Strauss and a group of his colleagues have identified at least ten social and psychological influences which may contribute to the development of "negative" symptoms. They have even suggested that *some* of these symptoms may reflect active coping strategies which provide solutions to the problems a person faces, and which may even help them to survive their often very difficult circumstances:

> Negative symptoms arise in many instances as responses to extremely difficult psychological and social situations. These symptoms may even serve to help the person with schizophrenia to survive [since they] may reflect active coping on the part of the patient [and] provide some psychological solutions for the problems patients encounter . . .[6]

The American Psychiatric Association has also acknowledged

that non-physical factors may contribute significantly to the development of "negative" symptoms. Thus, the most recent edition of the Diagnostic and Statistical Manual of Mental Disorders (DSM-IV) states that a number of factors may contribute to "negative" symptoms of schizophrenia including environmental under-stimulation, depression, demoralisation and persistent "positive" symptoms. The DSM-IV also acknowledges that medication side-effects *often* contribute to these problems and may be difficult to distinguish from "negative" symptoms related to other causes.[7]

In summary, it seems certain that in any given case a number of secondary factors which are *not* in themselves part of the "schizophrenic illness" may contribute significantly to the onset and persistence of "negative" symptoms. Prominent among these are likely to be a wide range of non-physical influences including psychological, emotional, social, and spiritual factors.

SCHIZOPHRENIA AND SENSITIVITY

Before proceeding to examine some of the specific factors that may contribute to the development of "negative" symptoms, it may be helpful to reflect on the nature of schizophrenia itself or – more importantly – on the nature of *people* who receive this diagnosis. Whilst a great deal of emphasis has been placed on the possible genetic factors that appear to predispose certain people to developing schizophrenia, in practical terms very little is known about how such genes might actually contribute to causing a person to develop psychotic symptoms in adult life. It is likely that one way in which this occurs may be related to the fact that *a major role of genes is to determine how an individual responds to his or her environment:*

> It is well known that genetic endowment does not determine an individual's traits (including the disorders he may develop); rather, the genes determine the responses of body and mind to environmental forces.[8]

Many investigators have shown that one very common characteristic of people who are predisposed to developing schizophrenia seems to be their *extreme sensitivity*. From a very early age such people may have a kind of "hypersensitivity" to sensory and emotional stimuli. It is possible that this sensitivity may be at least *partially* genetically determined. One standard psychiatric textbook states that:

> All [people with a diagnosis of schizophrenia] are, at least originally, more sensitive than the average person. It is likely that the increased sensitivity and heightened responsiveness to sensory and emotional stimulation is present . . . from an early age, possibly from birth. Schizophrenia may be characterised by a genetic hypersensitivity that leaves the [person] vulnerable to an overwhelming onslaught of stimuli from without and within.[9]

It is probable, of course, that genes are not the *only* factors responsible for a given person being extremely sensitive. Indeed, the very fact that about 90% of people who receive a diagnosis of schizophrenia have no known family history of the disorder strongly suggests that non-genetic factors are also involved.[10] Whatever may have contributed to anyone being hypersensitive, the end result is that such a person will have a tendency to experience life with a greater intensity than other people are inclined to. On the basis of her own experience Esso Leete has described what this may be like with respect to both sensory and interpersonal stimuli:

> For many individuals with a mental illness, we must learn to go through life experiencing our surroundings with a greater intensity than others do. Sounds are louder, lights brighter, colours more vibrant. These stimuli are distracting and confusing for us, and we are unable to filter their impact to lessen their effect. In addition, I believe we are more sensitive in an inter-personal sense as well. I have noticed that others like myself are easily able to pick up emotional non-verbal cues and feelings that may be "hidden".[11]

The existence of a long-standing hypersensitivity may partially help to explain how both "positive" and "negative" symptoms of schizophrenia develop. It is possible, for instance, that under certain circumstances a hypersensitive person may become overwhelmed by stimuli from inner and outer sources, with the final result being an "acute psychotic episode". On the other hand, extreme sensitivity may lead some people to withdraw or go into states of "shut-down" as a way to protect themselves from, and cope with, distressing and painful over-stimulation. Such people may consequently exhibit many of the typical "negative" symptoms.

The connection between sensitivity and withdrawal was recognised by Professor Eugen Bleuler early this century when he said:

> Particularly in the beginning of their illness, these patients quite consciously shun any contact with reality because their affects are so powerful that they must avoid everything which might arouse their emotions. The apathy toward the outer world is then a secondary one springing from a hypertrophied [i.e. excessively over-developed] sensitivity.[12]

It is important to note that although some "negative" symptoms may be seen as the end-product of a hypersensitive person's attempts to protect themselves by "shutting themselves off", such people still continue to be highly sensitive. Thus, even though some people with a high level of "negative" symptoms may *appear* to have become less responsive to the world around them, inwardly their original sensitivity remains, hidden behind what Professor Silvano Arieti has called an "armour of detachment":

> Although the [person] seems insensible and detached from the world, we must remember that he is affected by his environment even when no response is visible. It is because he is so sensitive that often he puts up this armour of detachment.[13]

Some of the specific ways in which self-protective withdrawal and "shut-down" may occur are discussed in detail in the following sections.

PSYCHOLOGICAL AND SOCIAL INFLUENCES THAT MAY CONTRIBUTE TO THE DEVELOPMENT OF "NEGATIVE" SYMPTOMS

In this section some of the many *non-physical* factors that might possibly contribute to a person with a diagnosis of schizophrenia developing "negative" symptoms are described. It is important to note that the relative importance of any of these influences may vary from one person to another, and that often a combination of several of them may be operating at any given time.

The following factors will be discussed in detail:

1 Institutionalisation
2 Self-Protective Withdrawal
3 Emotional "Shut-Down"
4 Cognitive (Mental) "Shut-Down"
5 Persistent Positive Symptoms
6 Post-Traumatic Stress Disorder (PTSD)
7 Post-Psychotic "Retreat"
8 Demoralisation
9 Depression
10 Living "At-A-Distance"

(1) *Institutionalisation*

Several decades ago it was recognised that people who spent long periods of time in hospital environments were often adversely affected by this experience. Long-stay patients, who usually had very little to do and few responsibilities, were observed to develop a syndrome (which came to be called "institutionalisation") characterised by apathy, disinterest, and a lack of initiative:

> Custodial institutional environments can so reduce stimulation and social demands that dysfunction in the form of negative symptoms such as decreased spontaneity, reduction in curiosity and ideation, reduced drive to interact, and blunted affect may result.[14]

Studies of long-stay hospitalised patients have shown that the severity of such "negative" symptoms as social withdrawal, flatness of affect, poverty of speech, slowness, and underactivity is *directly related to the length of time people have spent doing nothing.*[15] Sadly, the mistaken belief that people with a diagnosis of schizophrenia cannot really be helped probably contributed to these problems because such patients were often relegated to "second class" status, therapeutic neglect, and enforced idleness in some institutions.[16]

The so-called "deinstitutionalisation" movement of the 1960s, which developed largely as a result of growing concern about the possible negative effects of under-stimulating hospital environ-ments, has had a significant effect on reducing these problems. It is important to remember, however, that the syndrome of "institu-tionalisation" can occur in *any* environment which provides inadequate stimulation, responsibility, and structured activity. A person living in a boarding house or a hostel, or even in a family home, can also develop "negative" symptoms if they remain socially and mentally under-stimulated for excessively long periods:

> The extent to which similar deprivation is found in more extensive community-based programs is un-certain, but the naive hopes that deinstitutionalisation would eradicate this problem have been replaced by the knowledge that many patients live in circumstances pre-senting minimal interaction and social expectations.[17]

Simply removing a person from an under-stimulating hospital environment is not in itself enough to automatically reverse the effects of institutionalisation. In fact it has been said that it is sometimes easier to take the patient out of the hospital than it is to take the hospital out of the patient!

Despite these reservations it has been found that "negative" symptoms associated with long-term "institutionalisation" can often be significantly reduced simply by making the person's environment more stimulating.[18]

(2) *Self-Protective Withdrawal*

Among the various factors that contribute to the development of "negative" symptoms, some of the most important may be related to the way in which such patterns of behaviour may serve to protect a person from anxiety, distress and emotional pain.

Some people – perhaps especially those who are extremely sensitive – experience the world as being an often difficult and unsafe place. In such cases – and particularly if extreme levels of anxiety are generated by interactions with other people – a degree of protection may be provided by the use of social and emotional withdrawal. Social withdrawal primarily involves the active avoidance of other people and situations which are experienced as being too difficult or too stressful; emotional withdrawal involves avoidance of emotionally charged situations and/or the active suppression and "bottling up" of painful or distressing feelings.

It is likely that at one time or another *most* people use some degree of withdrawal as a way of coping with stress, anxiety, and excessive social demands. People who have a diagnosis of schizophrenia often seem to employ withdrawal to an *extreme* degree, possibly because their needs are extreme. In light of his research into schizophrenia, Professor Strauss has suggested that such "negative" symptoms as apathy, withdrawal, and even muteness:

> may reflect *a self-protective mechanism* that the person with [schizophrenia] uses to avoid the numerous discouragements and psychological assaults inflicted by the disorder, by society, and even by oneself. Withdrawal, apathy, and even muteness seem not unreasonable ways of protecting oneself from combined problems . . .[19]

Patricia Ruocchio has given a graphic description of how she used withdrawal to provide herself with a "safety shield" which helped to protect her from the extreme and unendurable anxiety and distress she experienced as a result of contact with others and the world:

> My safety shield, the wall of glass that separates and protects me from the world when it gets too frightening, has always been noted in [people with a diagnosis of schizophrenia] and is actually called by some the "wall of glass syndrome" . . . my fear of people, or as some have called it, "interpersonal terror", remains. . . . If I cannot actively make people around me disappear, I try to

disappear myself. I tend to withdraw more than attack, sometimes feeling myself melt into an inanimate object, actually becoming a chair or a wall. . . . there are many times that I feel so vulnerable that I need to pull away from the rest of the world. . . . The wall and the glass dome that isolated my world . . . made me the only being in existence.[20]

In keeping with its self-protective function Professor Strauss has noted that a person's degree of withdrawal often seems to increase when they are faced with significant changes in their environmental circumstances. When a person experiences a major change (such as discharge from hospital, for example), they may be observed to temporarily decrease the degree to which they relate to others or become involved in productive activity. This behaviour may be seen as being self-protective since it helps to reduce the amount of new demands on the person at a time when they are already faced with the many significant challenges involved with adjusting from being in hospital to being at home.

It is clear that the "wall of glass" described by Patricia Ruocchio serves both a protective and a defensive function: not only is the person behind it locked in, but – very importantly for the person feeling threatened – *others* are also locked out! An extreme degree of withdrawal may manifest as the "autism" which many psychiatrists have long considered to be a characteristic symptom of schizophrenia. Professor Eugen Bleuler, who introduced the term "schizophrenia" to psychiatry, recognised that even this form of profound withdrawal may have a self-protective purpose. In his seminal textbook he stated:

In part, (possibly entirely) the overt symptomatology [of schizophrenia] certainly represents the expression of a more or less unsuccessful attempt to find a way out of an intolerable situation. . . . *The patient renders reality harmless by refusing to let it touch him* (autism); he ignores it, isolates it, withdraws into his own thoughts. For these patients, autism has the same meaning as the walls of the monastery have for the monks, that the lonely desert has for some saints, and their studies for some scientists. In this respect, the difference between sickness and health is merely a quantitative one.[21]

In addition to protecting them from the *immediate* threats that they perceive in their environment, some people use withdrawal to avoid being exposed to the excessively stressful situations which sometimes seem to "trigger" psychotic episodes. Thus, over time, some people develop a kind of "sheltered" lifestyle which, by reducing their exposure to change and stress, may thereby help them to reduce their chances of "relapsing" into an acute psychotic state.[22]

(3) *Emotional "Shut-Down"*

Many "hypersensitive" people find that a certain degree of social and emotional withdrawal is quite an effective means of creating the "safety shield" they need. Sometimes, however, such withdrawal provides inadequate protection. In such cases an even more extreme coping strategy may sometimes be called into use.

Fortunately, nature has provided human beings with an automatic capacity to "switch off" their emotions and enter a state of "emotional anaesthesia" as a final means of escape from overwhelmingly painful feelings:

> The human capacity to blank oneself out and inwardly vanish as a form of protection is widespread. It may be that the capacity to blunt pain and anaesthetise oneself is a general characteristic of living beings. In human existence, this elemental capacity is raised to a new power. It can vary from a momentary going blank to a vast nullifying of the self.[23]

The existence of this capacity is evidenced by the fact that so-called "negative" symptoms are *not* confined to schizophrenia but are also found in many people who have had to endure severe and prolonged suffering. Survivors of concentration camps, for example, have described experiencing a profound "emotional numbness" which actually helped them to survive their ordeal. A psychiatrist who was imprisoned for several years in concentration camps during World War II has explained how the apathy and lack of feeling of prisoners provided a necessary "shell" which provided a means of self-protection and self-preservation under extremely difficult circumstances:

> Apathy, the blunting of the emotions and the feeling that one could not care any more, were the symptoms

arising during the second stage of the prisoner's psychological reactions, and which eventually made him insensitive to daily and hourly beatings. By means of this insensibility the prisoner soon surrounded himself with a very necessary protective shell.[24]

When viewed in this way, "negative" symptoms such as apathy and loss of feelings ("blunting of affect") may be seen as the end product of an extreme kind of self-protective emotional "shut-down" which occurs when a person is faced with intolerable suffering. Sources of pain which may provoke such a "shut-down" might be *internal* to the person (for example, paranoid delusions, persecuting "voices", emotional pain associated with stigma, rejection, or feelings of failure and guilt), or *external* (for example, hostility, criticism or intrusiveness of others, demands to perform beyond one's present ability). If no escape from painful feelings is possible, the only available solution may be to stop oneself from feeling altogether.

A vivid illustration of how such a state of "emotional shut-down" can help to protect a person is given in the case of a woman named Joan. After she was badly hurt by people Joan says: "I decided never to trust anyone again. For two years I closed myself up and froze so that I wouldn't feel anything". On another occasion, after she had been in a catatonic state of extreme withdrawal and "shut-down", Joan tells how a kind of "emotional suicide" had actually helped her to survive the very difficult situation she was experiencing:

> I tried to be dead and grey and motionless. . . . I felt as though I were in a bottle. I could feel that everything was outside and couldn't touch me. I had to die to keep from dying. I know that sounds crazy but one time a boy hurt my feelings very much and I wanted to jump in front of a subway. Instead I went a little catatonic so I wouldn't feel anything. (I guess you had to die emotionally or your feelings would have killed you.) [25]

At some point during their lives *most* people will probably experience a mild and transient degree of self-protective "emotional shut-down". For example, it is very common for people to experience a temporary state of emotional "numbness" whilst grieving the loss of a close friend or relative. Since it involves the damping down of *all* feelings, however, and not just painful ones, this natural coping mechanism can contribute to the development of "negative" symptoms if it is extreme or excessively prolonged. For some people, being in a state of prolonged "emotional shut-down" may seem like a preferable alternative to continuous and intense emotional pain, as Rae Unzicker has explained:

> Imagine the worst moment of your life. Extend it to an hour. A day. A year. Years on end, moments stacked up and lost forever. This is the stultifying process of madness. This is why mental patients look, act, and feel numb. To be in perpetual suspended animation is better than never-ending pain.[26]

Some researchers believe that the extreme degree of "blunting or flattening of affect" which characterises the most severe cases of schizophrenia may be related to a profound state of "emotional shut-down" which serves an important self-protective function.[27] In some instances, it may be that a state of "chronic" (i.e. prolonged) "emotional shut-down" is one of the major factors leading to so-called "chronic" schizophrenia.

(4) *Cognitive (Mental) "Shut-Down"*

People who are experiencing high levels of stress may use withdrawal in order to reduce their level of stimulation to a more manageable level. Such a coping strategy may not always be possible, however, nor is it necessarily always totally effective. In such cases a type of self-protective *mental "shut-down"* sometimes automatically occurs. Many people have had a mild experience of this kind when their mind has suddenly "gone blank" when they have been under great pressure. For example, such a temporary "mental block" sometimes occurs during stressful examinations or whilst a person is undergoing a high-pressure interview.

People who are extremely sensitive sometimes feel as if they are in danger of being overwhelmed by the amount of stimulation going on in and around them. If the myriad thoughts, feelings, images, memories and sounds – from inside and outside – threaten to throw a person into a state of utter disorganisation and confusion (which may herald the onset of an acute psychotic episode), a protective mechanism may *automatically* begin to operate to quickly reduce their level of stimulation.

For example, if their state of mental confusion and distractability threatens to reach an extreme level, some people experience their mind suddenly going "blank" or empty. They may even feel as if they have temporarily gone into a kind of trance. This state of "trance" or mental "blanking out" may be the result of a self-protective reaction to excessive stimulation which is rather like the automatic switching off of an overloaded electrical circuit by a circuit breaker. An example of this defence mechanism is given by a person who described how his mind sometimes suddenly went blank when he became overstimulated by everything going on around him:

> It's like a temporary blackout – like being in a vacuum. I just get cut off from outside things and go into another world. This happens when the tension starts to mount until it bursts in my brain. It has to do with what is going on around me – taking in too much of my surroundings – vital not to miss anything. I can't shut things out of my mind and everything closes in on me. It stops me thinking and then the mind goes a blank and everything gets switched off. [28]

Some researchers have suggested that there might be specific in-built mechanisms which help to protect hypersensitive individuals from "stimulus overload" by automatically switching their nervous system into a state of "protective inhibition".[29] This can be thought of as being a bit like temporarily turning down the "volume" of the electrical signals within the person's nervous system. Whilst the operation of this mechanism can protect a hypersensitive person by reducing their excessive sensitivity to external and internal stimulation, the *generalised* reduction of activity in their nervous system may also contribute to slowed thinking, lowered motivation, and a degree of emotional dulling.

(5) *Persistent "Positive" Symptoms*

Sometimes, "negative" symptoms may develop as a direct result of a person's attempts to cope with persistent "positive" psychotic symptoms such as delusions, hallucinations, or disturbed thinking. For example, a person with persecutory delusions ("paranoia") who feels that their life could be in danger if they leave their room or speak to anyone may keep away from others and refuse to speak. In such a case the person's continued need for "social withdrawal" and "uncommunicativeness" is motivated by their desire to protect themselves from what they perceive to be very real dangers. Similarly, a person who hears "voices" which continually mock or criticise them for doing certain things (e.g. trying to make themselves look nice by attending to their grooming) may stop doing those things so that the "voices" will finally leave them in peace. People who hear "voices" which they experience as being good and helpful, or which provide them with some kind of enjoyable companionship, may sometimes become so deeply engrossed in these voices that they become less interested in the world around them.[30]

Many of the strategies which people use in their attempts to cope with persistent "positive" symptoms may be obvious to others (e.g. social withdrawal). Sometimes, however, such strategies may be occurring on a purely *internal* level. As an example, Elizabeth Farr has described how she deliberately attempted to stop herself from thinking because she believed that other people were able to listen in on her thoughts:

> Sometimes my thoughts were audibly loud and I began to think that other people could hear what I was thinking. I used to think that I could hear my thought waves being broadcast over speakers when I was in a lecture. I had absolutely no sense of privacy. My innermost thoughts were broadcast to the world. I began to spend a lot of time and energy trying to block my thoughts, particularly the thoughts I wanted to keep to myself. ... There was really a lot going on inside me, but it must have seemed to outsiders that my head was quite vacant.[31]

Whilst her attempt to block her thoughts helped Elizabeth Farr to regain a sense of privacy, it also produced a "negative" symptom very similar to that which psychiatrists refer to as "thought blocking". ("Thought broadcasting" and "thought blocking" are both considered to be common symptoms of schizophrenia.)

Although it is often assumed that most people who are receiving regular neuroleptic ("anti-psychotic") medication will generally be free of "positive" symptoms, research has shown that this is not necessarily the case. One recent study revealed that a substantial proportion of people still had "positive" symptoms at discharge from hospital: 51.0% had persistent delusions, 31.4% were experiencing hallucinations, and 25.5% had formal thought disorder.[32]

The research of Professor Ian Falloon has led him to conclude that a large proportion of observable "negative" symptoms can indeed be directly attributed to the existence of persistent "positive" symptoms, although the fact that the person is continuing to experience "positive" symptoms may not have even been recognised:

> In a careful survey, in which patients were interviewed in their own homes after treatment of florid episodes of schizophrenia, 92% of patients with significant "negative" symptoms revealed persistent delusions, hallucinations or thought interference. In many cases the patients were able to describe how their ["positive"] symptoms contributed to the "negative" features, especially the continued need for social withdrawal. . . . it should be noted that a substantial proportion of these [patients] disclosed the persistence of their ["positive"] symptoms only when systematically questioned in their own homes, and were reported as consistently free of ["positive"] psychotic symptoms at their aftercare clinics.[33]

When neuroleptic medications are effective in eliminating or reducing the intensity of "positive" symptoms such as delusions and hallucinations, any "negative" symptoms related to them may also diminish as the person feels less need to cope by withdrawing or avoiding people. Unfortunately, however, the side-effects of neuroleptic medications sometimes contribute to "negative" symptoms such as loss of motivation or emotional flatness (see page 41 for a detailed discussion of medication issues).

(6) *Post-Traumatic Stress Disorder (PTSD)*
It has long been recognised that a person who has had an extremely traumatic experience (such as violent personal assault, torture, military combat, serious motor vehicle accident, incarceration in a concentration camp, hostage situation, etc.)

may develop a number of characteristic symptoms following such experience. Collectively these symptoms are now referred to as *Post-Traumatic Stress Disorder*, or PTSD for short.[34]

PTSD symptoms usually begin within three months of the traumatic experience (although there can be a delay of months or even years before they begin to appear). Complete recovery from PTSD may occur within 3 months in about half of people affected ("acute PTSD"), but many others may have symptoms which persist for longer than 12 months after the original trauma ("chronic PTSD"). Typical PTSD symptoms may include the following:

- Distressing recollections of the traumatic event (e.g. intrusive thoughts, recurrent distressing dreams, flashbacks);
- Persistent avoidance of any thoughts, feelings, or conversations about the traumatic event;
- Persistent symptoms of increased arousal (e.g. irritability, difficulty falling or staying asleep, poor concentration);
- Numbing of general responsiveness.

The last symptom, involving a diminished responsiveness to the external world, has been referred to as "*psychic numbing*" or "*emotional anaesthesia*" (this is similar to the "emotional shutdown" referred to earlier). According to the American Psychiatric Association it usually begins soon after the traumatic event and may manifest itself in the following specific ways:

> The individual may complain of having markedly diminished interest or participation in previously enjoyed activities, of feeling detached or estranged from other people, or of having markedly reduced ability to feel emotions (especially those associated with intimacy, tenderness, and sexuality). The individual may have a sense of a foreshortened future (e.g. not expecting to have a career, marriage, children, or a normal life span).[35]

The "numbing of general responsiveness" characteristic of PTSD closely resembles the "negative" symptoms of schizophrenia in many ways, although it is only relatively recently that the possible connection between the two has begun to be recognised by mental health professionals. A number of researchers have now shown that for *some* people the experience of psychosis and/or subsequent hospitalisation may indeed be sufficiently traumatising to provoke the development of a full-blown Post-Traumatic Stress Disorder with its accompanying "psychic numbing".[36]

In a recent study, PTSD symptoms were found to be common during the post-psychotic recovery phase: 46% of people had these symptoms 4 months after an acute psychotic episode, and 35% still had them after 11 months.[37] Some researchers have suggested that some degree of PTSD should be *expected* following most, if not all, episodes of psychosis. In this view, the real question is to what extent the "negative" symptoms following acute psychosis are *psychologically* caused manifestations of a Post-Traumatic Stress Disorder.[38]

A very important finding of the research of Professor McGorry and his colleagues[37] was that some people found the experience of involuntary hospitalisation (often involving enforced medication or seclusion) to be even *more* traumatising than the experience of psychosis itself! On the basis of her personal experiences and observations, one leading American consumer advocate has expressed the following opinion:

> It is important to understand that we are faced with recovering not just from mental illness, but also from the effects of being labelled mentally ill. I believe many of us emerge from mental institutions with full-blown post-traumatic stress disorders that are a direct result of the trauma and abuse we may have experienced or witnessed in mental institutions or in community based programs.[39]

Whatever the specific causes of PTSD may be for any particular individual it is highly likely that this frequently unrecognised post-psychotic syndrome, with its accompanying "psychic numbing", may contribute significantly to the development of "negative" symptoms associated with schizophrenia. If this view is correct, providing timely and effective treatment of PTSD – for instance, by means of supportive counselling of the kind provided to victims of natural disasters, serious assault, combat trauma, etc. – could prove to be a vital component in any comprehensive treatment of people who have experienced psychosis.[37]

(7) *Post-Psychotic "Retreat"*

Immediately following the experience of a psychotic episode many people go through a prolonged period during which they feel flat and apathetic and are unmotivated and socially withdrawn. Although this state is sometimes diagnosed as post-psychotic depression (see Section 9, below), some researchers believe that it is best understood as an *essential phase of recuperation and restitution*.[40] Such a recuperative phase provides a recently psychotic person with much-needed "time out" during which they can slowly and gradually begin the process of re-establishing their psychological, emotional and social equilibrium which has been deeply disturbed by the profound personal crisis of psychosis.

Professor Strauss has suggested that this period of temporary withdrawal may provide the recovering person with a much-needed opportunity for "a long rest in a protected environment". As such, it may be a *natural and essential part of the healing process*, although it is not always recognised as such:

> [Post-psychotic retreat] especially when it occurs immediately after hospital discharge, appears to reflect a pathological withdrawal – a negative symptom; but it may actually be a mechanism to prevent recurrence of positive symptoms by providing respite from the demands of interaction with the environment . . . especially when it is followed, as it often is, by a subsequent step up to a new higher level of function, [post-psychotic retreat] might be viewed as a coping mechanism.[41]

A period of post-psychotic "retreat" (which is sometimes called "regression") could be thought of as the "calm" following the psychotic "storm". This period may last for several months, during which time "negative"-type symptoms are often quite pronounced and may include:[42]

- feelings of weakness, tiredness, lack of energy;
- excessive sleeping during the day;
- desire to be alone;
- loss of interest in activity, profound passivity;
- feelings of emptiness, aloneness, and unlovability;
- partial "blunting" or complete "flattening" of affect.

Feelings of extreme fragility and vulnerability are especially common, as Mark Vonnegut has described:

> When I was finally released from the hospital, I bore little resemblance to the dynamo of assertion I had been . . . I had nothing but a feeling of extreme fragility and vulnerability and a little hope that some day things would be different. I didn't adjust well to being fragile and vulnerable. [My girlfriend] Virginia or my parents or anyone else could break me inadvertently. Just a slight human clumsiness and "snap".[43]

A sensitive understanding of this phase in recovery shows that things are not always what they may appear to be. Thus, even though very little may *seem* to be happening whilst a person is temporarily "cocooned" within themselves, subtle changes may still be occurring, hidden from view. For example, the person may be gradually getting used to being with people again, slowly building up their self-confidence, and gathering strength for the challenge of returning to life in the world once more. Thus these quiet phases of "retreat" may provide essential "time out" during which important processes of recuperation and healing are able to take place.[44]

Although a person who is going through a period of post-psychotic retreat may appear to have many "negative" symptoms, no specific treatment is required, other than a temporary reduction of performance expectations and consistent but *non-intrusive* support. In many cases the person will gradually begin to emerge from this transient, self-limiting state after a few months:

> If the patient has recently recovered from a psychotic episode, one might anticipate a period, usually lasting several months, in which negative symptoms are pronounced. There is no specific treatment for this condition. A supportive therapeutic relationship, non-pressuring but consistent, is considered to be important. In addition, the patient and family should be informed about this aspect of the post-psychotic state and encouraged to persevere.[45]

(8) *Demoralisation*

In many cases, one of the most important factors contributing to the development of "negative" symptoms can be simply described as *demoralisation*.[46] This involves the wearing down of a person's self-confidence and hopefulness to such a degree that they begin to feel that there is no point in continuing to struggle any longer.

Sooner or later most people who experience severe problems which persist for a long time could eventually become demoralised. People coping with serious physical illnesses or injuries, for instance, often begin to feel hopeless at times during their ordeal. As an example, Tony Moore, who suffered multiple serious injuries in a motor car accident, has described his own experience of total demoralisation during a long period of confinement to bed in hospital:

> It feels as though someone is shifting the finishing line of a marathon further and further away as one stumbles towards it exhausted and bereft. I am so tired, so incapable and unwilling to do battle of any sort. My only option is to become quiet and withdrawn – it's the only way to cope. I must subtract all personal involvement from any additional stresses and leave them behind me. ... I will just withdraw. ... All joys seem to have vanished. That is the worst damage that has been done. I have no appetite for the new adventure. I feel alone. ... The accident removed the chance for me to determine my life. When everyday events caused further erosion of my self-determination, it was tempting to surrender completely from the fight. It was the only time in my life when suicide seemed a solution.[47]

If it is sufficiently intense, demoralisation might induce temporary "negative" symptoms in virtually *anyone*. Given the many difficulties they must face, people who have a diagnosis of schizophrenia are likely to be especially prone to becoming demoralised to one degree or another at times. Patricia Deegan has described how a "paralysis of the will" can result when all hope seems lost, and giving up seems inevitable:

> For months I sat in a chair in my family's living room, smoking cigarettes and waiting until it was 8.00pm so I

could go back to bed. At this time even the simplest of
tasks were overwhelming. I remember being asked to
come into the kitchen to help knead some bread
dough. I got up, went into the kitchen, and looked at
the dough for what seemed an eternity. Then I walked
back to my chair and wept. The task seemed overwhelming to me. Later I learned the reason for this:
when one lives without hope (when one has given up)
the willingness to "do" is paralysed as well.[48]

Professor Strauss has concluded that demoralisation itself is an
important – perhaps even a key factor – in understanding
"negative" symptoms.[49] Others have agreed with his opinion:

Withdrawal, that is to say, isolation and alienation, and
the associated phenomena of amotivation, apathy, and
anhedonia are partly a manifestation of this
demoralised condition. Indeed, much of what has
been described as the "negative symptom syndrome" is
attributable to demoralisation . . .[50]

Among the range of factors that may contribute to
demoralisation in people with a diagnosis of schizophrenia the
following are often especially important:

(a) *Stigmatisation and Labelling*
For a range of complex reasons the diagnosis of schizophrenia
probably has more stigma attached to it than that of practically
any other illness, physical or mental. This stigma inevitably has a
very detrimental effect on a person, making it difficult for them
to feel good about themselves, and reducing their chances of
being accepted by others.

Professor Joseph Zubin has concluded that stigmatisation and
labelling do have a very powerful influence on people who have
been diagnosed. Professor Zubin believes their effect is so
powerful, in fact, that it is the *social consequences* of being labelled,
rather than schizophrenia in itself, which is largely responsible
for the "negative" symptoms:

Negative symptoms are neither an inevitable nor an
intrinsic feature of schizophrenic disorders. [Rather,
they are] a social consequence of having been

identified, labelled, and treated as schizophrenic by medical specialists, relatives, close friends, and other members of the patient's social network.[51]

Esso Leete's own experience led her to make these comments regarding the pernicious effects of being "labelled":

> Life with a psychiatric diagnosis is difficult. I can talk but I may not be heard. I can make suggestions, but they may not be taken seriously. I can voice my thoughts, but they may be seen as delusions. I can recite experiences, but they may be interpreted as fantasies. To be a patient or even an ex-client is to be discounted. Our label is a reality that never leaves us; it gradually shapes an identity that is hard to shed.[52]

(b) *Pessimistic "Therapeutic" Messages*

Professor Strauss believes that some of the most common messages that are given to people with a diagnosis of schizophrenia may contribute in a substantial way to their eventual demoralisation. Sensitive and vulnerable individuals are likely to be *especially* prone to having their hopes and self-confidence undermined if pessimistic scenarios are described for their future lives:

> The contributions of treatment interventions to apathy and withdrawal may also be particularly powerful in schizophrenia. Some of the most common treatment efforts may inadvertently create the opposite effect from the one intended. Patients with schizophrenia are often told that they have a disease like diabetes. They are told that they will have the disease all their lives, that it involves major and permanent functional impairment, and that they will have a life-long need for medication.[53]

Ironically, one of the most powerfully demoralising messages of all may be that "negative" symptoms are – in their entirety – a permanent and essentially untreatable part of schizophrenia which a person can do nothing about and which they must simply accept and learn to put up with.

(c) *Learned Helplessness*

In time some people gradually develop the belief that they are nothing but a passive "victim" of schizophrenia who has very little control over what will happen to them. The belief that they have been robbed of the power to choose their direction in life leaves some people feeling that, rather than being in the driver's seat of their lives, they are now merely a helpless passenger. In many cases, Patricia Deegan believes, the effects of such "learned helplessness" can be even *more* damaging than the original psychotic disturbance itself:

> One learns to become helpless in situations in which one has no control and, no matter what one does, it doesn't really matter. The syndrome of learned helplessness creates deficits in three important spheres of human functioning, including motivation (i.e., I don't care because what I do doesn't matter anyway); cognition (i.e., my actions fail to have an impact here and everywhere else, too); and emotion (i.e., I give up trying and experience apathy/depression/anxiety). The symptoms of learned helplessness include apathy, resignation, anger, submissiveness, depression, anxiety, withdrawal, and compliance. These symptoms are often mistaken by mental health professionals to be the so-called "negative symptoms" of psychotic disorders.[54]

(d) *Guilt and Shame*

Associated with the stigma referred to above, it is common for people to experience feelings of shame or guilt. Sometimes these feelings are related to things the person has said or done whilst they were in a psychotic state, or even to some of the thoughts, feelings, or wishes they may have held at that time. In addition, because Western societies generally have extremely negative attitudes toward "mental illness", the very fact that a person has been psychotic may cause feelings of shame. People may tell themselves things like "I should have been strong enough to control my own mind", or "A strong-willed person wouldn't get schizophrenia". Irrational beliefs such as these can contribute in a powerful way to creating intensely painful guilt feelings and, eventually, a sense of personal defeat.

(e) *Fear of Relapse*

The fear that they might become psychotic again at some unpredictable time in the future is a reality which lurks in the back of many people's minds, inhibiting their confidence and motivation. This fear causes some people to use protective social withdrawal *excessively* in the hope that they will be able to avoid trouble by eliminating as many sources of stress from their lives as possible. It may also cause others (such as family or friends) to become overly protective. One person who experienced a persistent fear of "relapse" described the effect it had on his motivation to do things:

> What I found tiring, at times, was the effort involved in making myself do things. For example, to get out of a chair and go for a walk required a great deal of effort. I seemed to be apathetic, perhaps because of the feeling of having to start yet again to build my life fearing that, even when I have rebuilt it, it may again collapse.[55]

Such feelings are especially likely if a person is unaware of the many things they can learn to do for themselves to reduce their chances of experiencing "relapse" (see Part Two).

(f) *Loss of Direction and Purpose*

The experience of psychosis has a powerful impact on a person and inevitably changes their life. For many people this occurs very forcefully, often at quite a young age. Inevitably, many questions arise regarding one's identity and future direction. Often, a period of grief and mourning occurs as earlier life plans are given up and self-identity undergoes profound changes. Whilst struggling to come to terms with these issues feelings of loss and despair are very common. As with the long-term unemployed, many people may begin to experience their lives as lacking any sense of journey or purpose, as Marcia Lovejoy has described:

> Although I had just turned nineteen I saw myself as incurably ill, as someone who would always need to be taken care of by others. . . . I left the hospital and tried to fit into my new role as sick and retired from active living, but I was overwhelmed by the emptiness of my

future. I became increasingly afraid of myself and my
feelings ... I felt ashamed, helpless, useless, and
frightened. My experiences in the community only
confirmed these feelings.[56]

(g) *Physical/Mental/Emotional Exhaustion*

Many people find that their on-going struggles require a great
deal of energy. A huge amount of mental and emotional energy
can be "burnt up" in a short time during a psychotic episode, and
it can take a long time for a person to "recharge their batteries"
afterwards. (Some of this "recharging" may occur during a period
of undisturbed post-psychotic "retreat", as described earlier.) Day-
to-day coping can also be a drain, especially if a person has not
developed effective coping skills. At times, a lot of energy can be
expended suppressing painful feelings, or simply in the effort to
"hold it all together". Such mental and emotional drains on
energy are likely to be even more of a problem for anyone who
eats poorly, sleeps irregularly, avoids exercise, and smokes too
much since all of these habits are likely to further erode a
person's available energy.

Anyone who is deeply affected by these (and possibly other)
demoralising influences may undergo the profound "faltering of
the spirit" that Patricia Deegan believes is a common experience
for everyone who struggles with serious and prolonged psychological and emotional problems. As she looked back at where she
herself had been years before, Deegan was able to see what she
had been through:

> And as I watch her, I know it is not so much mental
> illness that I am observing. I am witnessing the flame of
> a human spirit faltering. She is losing the will to live.
> She is not suicidal – but she wants to die because
> nothing seems worth living for. Her hopes, her dreams,
> and her aspirations have been shattered. She sees no
> way to achieve the valued roles she had once dreamed
> of. Her future has been reduced to the prognosis of
> doom she has been given. Her past is slipping away like
> a dream that belonged to someone else. Her present is
> empty but for the pungent cigarette smoke that fills the
> void like a veiled spectre. No, this is not mental illness

I am seeing. I am seeing a young woman whose hope for living a full and valuable life has been shattered. She feels herself to be among the living dead and her spirit is wavering under the weight of it all.[57]

In this situation, Patricia Deegan has explained, *giving up may actually be experienced as a solution.* This is so, she says, because giving up helps to numb the pain of despair. Now, instead of asking "why and how can I go on?", and finding no answers, the person may quietly let go of all possible hope and simply allow themselves to begin settling into a state of ever-deepening apathy:

> The answer, the only way to survive this kind of living death, was to give up. The professionals called it apathy and lack of motivation. They blamed it on the illness. But they don't understand that giving up is a highly motivated and highly goal-directed behaviour. For us, giving up was a way of surviving. Giving up, refusing to hope, not trying, not caring: all of these were ways of trying to protect the last fragile traces of our spirit and our selfhood from undergoing another crushing.[58]

(9) *Depression*

Given the very many difficulties with which they are faced it is hardly surprising that depression is a common problem among people who have a diagnosis of schizophrenia. An episode of quite severe depression often occurs immediately following a psychotic episode, as well as at other times.[59]

Among the many psychological and social factors that might contribute to a person becoming depressed are: the stigma of "mental illness", disruption of work and career, feelings of failure and rejection, loss of friends, reduced self-confidence, damaged self-esteem, and loss of hope for the future. Research has also shown that some people being treated with neuroleptic medications can develop a particular type of depression (called "akinetic depression") which is related to the side-effects of these drugs.[60] (Medication issues are discussed in detail on pages 41–46.)

Some of the symptoms of depression – such as loss of motivation, lack of interest in doing things, slowing of thought and speech, lack of emotional expression (mask-like face, reduced "body language") – can closely resemble "negative" symptoms, and may consequently be mistaken for them. The resemblance is only superficial, however, and it is often possible for an experienced person to tell the difference. In particular, whereas a person with severe "negative" symptoms is more likely to complain of feeling "empty", "stuck" or "blank", someone who is depressed often experiences quite strong feelings – albeit painful ones. Thus, depressed people often complain of feeling incompetent, defective, or sinful, and they may feel guilty about being a burden to others, or about things they have done or failed to do. Often they have strong feelings of hopelessness and worthlessness, and a feeling that anything they do will fail. If the depression is especially severe, suicidal thoughts may occur, and in some cases may even lead to self-destructive acts.

Because depression is such a common problem for people living with schizophrenia it is likely that *in some cases what appear to be "negative" symptoms are, in fact, mainly symptoms of depression.*[61] In other cases, however, depression might only be partially responsible for "negative" symptoms, whilst some of the factors described earlier play a more important part.

(10) *Living "At-A-Distance"*

In addition to the factors listed above there may sometimes be another, somewhat different, set of influences which contribute to patterns of behaviour which, though superficially resembling certain "negative" symptoms, are probably more correctly seen as reflecting a person's individual interpersonal "style" and way of being in the world.

One of the biggest problems facing those who attempt to research "negative" symptoms is that nobody can really say what is "normal" when it comes to anyone's level of motivation, degree of emotional expressiveness, manner of interacting with other people, and so on. This is so because everybody is a unique individual who develops and adapts to life in their own way, according to their own personal characteristics and life experiences. Appreciating this fact highlights the possibility that some people may develop a personal style of life which, while it could be seen as involving some "negative" symptoms, might be for that particular person an acceptable – perhaps even a preferred – way of being.

As an example, some people with a diagnosis of schizophrenia deliberately adopt a "sheltered" lifestyle which, though appearing from the outside to involve such "negative" symptoms as passivity and avoidance, allows them to remain closer to the rich inner world which is the truest source of meaning and identity in their lives. Some researchers have referred to such a lifestyle as one characterised by *"positive withdrawal"*.[62]

As was explained at the beginning of this book, people who receive a diagnosis of schizophrenia are often particularly sensitive. It is possible that this extreme degree of sensitivity may partly be related to genetically determined characteristics. In any case, it means that from a very early age such people must learn to develop a way of living which will adequately protect them from the over-stimulation to which their unique sensitivity makes them prone. For some highly sensitive people the solution is found in adopting an "at-a-distance" lifestyle.

The philosopher Schopenhauer liked to compare human beings to hedgehogs huddling together in the cold: they like to huddle close enough to stay warm, he said, but not so close that they prick one another! Somewhat like hedgehogs, people also have "spikes" of different lengths. For whatever reason, some people appear to have especially short ones. In order to feel most comfortable, such people seem to have a special need for "personal space" and a bit of distance from others: not being too far away, on the one hand, but not being too close, on the other. People of this kind are sometimes described as being "introverted". All this really means is that they are more strongly attuned to their *inner* world of thoughts, imagination and feeling than they are to the outer world of physical reality, in which more "extroverted" people feel very much at home. Because modern Western societies are generally very "extroverted", those people who have an "introverted" nature are often judged harshly. It may even be implied that there is something fundamentally wrong or unhealthy about their particular style of personal adjustment.

Professor Silvano Arieti has described the development of a highly sensitive person who – like a hedgehog with especially short "spikes" – is able to live most comfortably only if they are not forced into being too close to, or too much involved with, other people. Precisely because they are so sensitive, such people may experience ordinary, quite "normal" emotions very intensely.

Their anxiety levels, for example, may become almost unbearable at times. Consequently, they must use a range of self-protective manoeuvres. As they grow up, such people may always remain somewhat aloof and emotionally detached from others. However, although appearing outwardly to be less emotional, less concerned, and less involved than the average person, inwardly a quite different reality may exist, as Professor Arieti has described:

> Secretly he remains very sensitive, but he has learned to avoid anxiety and anger in two ways: by making himself as inconspicuous as possible, putting physical distance between himself and situations that are apt to arouse these feelings; and by repressing emotions. The physical distance is maintained by avoiding relationships with other people or refraining from actions that may displease others. The child, and later the adolescent, becomes quiet.[63]

Such people, who have sometimes been described by psychiatrists as having a "schizoid" personality, were once thought to be prone to becoming overtly schizophrenic later in life. It is possible, however, that an "at-a-distance" lifestyle may actually help to *reduce* the risk of psychosis for some people by protecting them from the stresses which too close an involvement with other people and with life generally may cause them.

The important point is that sometimes what may appear to be "negative" symptoms – such as aloofness or emotional detachment – may actually be *long-standing personality characteristics* which developed well before a diagnosis of schizophrenia was ever given. Such characteristics, developing in an exceptionally sensitive individual from an early age, may have important "survival value" for the person, and reflect his or her own style of adjustment and unique way of being in the world.[64]

"NEGATIVE" SYMPTOMS AND SENSITIVITY TO THE SOCIAL ENVIRONMENT

Researchers who have studied the level of physiological arousal (as reflected in the heart rate and sweat gland activity) of people with so-called "chronic schizophrenia" have found that the most withdrawn and least motivated individuals often have the *highest* level of arousal. This seemingly paradoxical finding has been interpreted as suggesting that the socially withdrawn person is in fact *more* sensitive to his or her environment than a so-called "normal" person would be.[65]

Possibly because of the way in which their constitutional hypersensitivity influenced the way they experienced their formative relationships, many people who eventually receive a diagnosis of schizophrenia seem to have an *exquisite sensitivity* to their social environment. In particular, they are often especially sensitive to the feelings that exist between themselves and the other people they are with (the "emotional atmosphere"). One person explained how heightened sensitivity early in life can lead to conflicts which may leave behind "emotional scars":

> Besides the day-to-day stress ... there are emotional problems that have evolved and accumulated over the course of the patient's life ... I believe that several incidents during my lifetime occurred because of something "different" about me ... A child destined to become schizophrenic must deal not only with the seeds of illness within himself but also with the attitudes of others toward his "idiosyncrasies", whether these feelings are voiced openly or subtly manifested in everyday life. ... the scars of emotional confusion remain, felt perhaps more deeply by a greater sensitivity and vulnerability.[66]

If they are carried over into adulthood, such "emotional scars" sometimes seem to *increase* the person's pre-existing sensitivity. In extreme cases it may almost seem as though such people have a kind of "emotional radar" which is finely tuned to pick up the slightest nuances of criticism or "put down" by others. Some people may become especially vulnerable to being upset by any criticism or hostility which they believe is being directed at them. In circumstances involving high levels of stress they may even tend to become "paranoid" as a result of their tendency to exaggerate or misinterpret the motives and behaviour of others.

Feeling unfairly criticised or "put down" is difficult enough for a person with an ordinary degree of sensitivity to handle; it is likely to be *especially* difficult for anyone whose extreme sensitivity makes them particularly "thin skinned" and vulnerable. In circumstances which they experience as threatening, such people may resort to using some of the coping strategies described earlier (such as self-protective withdrawal and emotional "shut-down"). This might occur in *any* environment or situation in which the person is exposed to harsh criticism, hostility, unrealistic demands and expectations (i.e. beyond their present capabilities), emotional intrusiveness (for example, "smothering", excessive anxiety about minor matters, over-protectiveness).

People who have a diagnosis of schizophrenia might be exposed to some or all of these potentially harmful attitudes in many different situations including: in-patient and out-patient treatment settings, psychosocial rehabilitation programmes, their workplace, and even their own homes (including their family home).

The Emotional Climate of the Family

Generally speaking, people are usually somewhat more sensitive to criticism which comes from their relatives than they are to criticism which comes from non-family members. This fact has some very important implications for people living with schizophrenia, especially if "negative" symptoms have become a problem.

Many families continue to show remarkably supportive, tolerant and accepting attitudes towards a relative who has a diagnosis of schizophrenia.[67] Desirable attitudes such as these are not always easy for family members to maintain, however, particularly if they face a daily struggle with problems such as their diagnosed relative's continuing uncommunicativeness, lack of emotion, low level of motivation, and isolative behaviour.

Indeed, research has shown that these very behaviours are actually *more* likely to elicit criticism from family members than are "positive" symptoms such as delusions and hallucinations.[68] They may even be perceived as signs of the person's irresponsibility, deliberate avoidance, or outright laziness.

Undoubtedly some people with a diagnosis of schizophrenia *do* allow themselves to become increasingly lazy and irresponsible. In many instances, however, it is likely that at least some of the "negative" symptom behaviours are actually outward manifestations of the person's attempts to protect themselves from excessive demands, over-stimulation, and emotional pain. This is especially likely to be the case during the first few years following diagnosis, when the person has not yet had time to develop a "thick skin", emotionally speaking.

Family members who do not understand their diagnosed relative's need for a tortoise-like shell of self-protective withdrawal and emotional "shut-down" may – quite unwittingly – contribute to the development of a vicious circle. This can happen because a person who has become withdrawn and unresponsive may retreat *even further* into themselves if they feel excessively pressured, criticised or intruded upon by caring family members intent on encouraging them to "come out of their shell".

A tolerant and non-critical attitude, on the other hand, may help to prevent such a vicious circle from beginning. The finding that positive and supportive family communications can help to reduce some "negative" symptoms[69] highlights the importance of always working to create and maintain a comfortable emotional climate for *everyone* within the family home.

(NOTE: Some specific practical guidelines for family members are outlined in Part Two.)

The Optimal Social Environment

Anyone who is significantly slower, quieter, and less emotionally expressive than others may easily become the target of hostility and criticism. For example, overly-enthusiastic rehabilitation programmes may have unrealistic expectations about how quickly a person should be progressing and subtly criticise someone who is seen as being "too slow"; unsympathetic workmates might accuse a slow person of not pulling their weight; friends may interpret a person's lack of interest in socialising as a sign of unfriendliness; mental health professionals may feel frustrated at a client's very slow rate of progress, and some may even interpret a lack of emotional responsiveness as a personal rejection. In any of these situations, subtle – and sometimes not so subtle – anger, blame and criticism may be directed at the person. Unfortunately, such reactions are only likely to compound the original problem.

Professor Wing has noted that many people with a diagnosis of schizophrenia often seem to be highly sensitive to the effects of both emotional over- and under-stimulation. On the basis of his research into the way that a person's social environment can influence both their "positive" and "negative" symptoms, Professor Wing has suggested that a balance must always be found between *too much* stressful stimulation on the one hand, and *too little*, on the other. In order for this to be achieved, he believes:

> The optimal social environment is structured, with neutral (i.e. not highly emotionally involved) stimulation to perform up to achievable standards, with little necessity for complex decision-making but with some degree of control over the amount of social stimulation left in the [person's] own hands.[70]

In these optimal circumstances, Professor Wing feels, the diagnosed person is more likely to develop feelings of trust and confidence in family members and mental health professionals. In addition, their need for the protective "stress buffering" effects of neuroleptic medications are likely to be minimal.

NEUROLEPTIC MEDICATIONS AND "NEGATIVE" SYMPTOMS

Neuroleptic ("anti-psychotic") medications have become the mainstay of the medical treatment of schizophrenia. On the plus side, these drugs can often provide people with considerable relief from painful and disturbing "positive" symptoms such as delusions, hallucinations and thought disorder. Effective treatment with neuroleptic drugs may even help to reduce some "negative" type symptoms, such as those related to withdrawal due to persistent "positive" symptoms or high levels of anxiety. They may also have a prophylactic effect, in the sense that they may significantly reduce the chances of "relapse" for people who are at risk of becoming psychotic again.

As with all drugs, however, adverse or unwanted effects (which are commonly referred to as "side-effects") can sometimes be a significant problem. Unfortunately, *some of the side-effects of neuroleptic drugs can mimic or compound problems with "negative" symptoms.* The American Psychiatric Association has recently acknowledged that neuroleptic medications *often* cause side-effects which closely resemble the affective flattening and loss of motivation which are commonly found in people who have a diagnosis of schizophrenia.[71] And, in addition to producing some "negative" symptoms, neuroleptic drugs may also contribute to a worsening of "negative" symptoms which originally developed as a result of other factors. For example, it is possible that the loss of motivation related to "emotional shut-down" or demoralisation may become even more severe if a person is receiving prolonged neuroleptic treatment – especially if excessively large dosages are used.[72]

Because of these dangers, great care needs to be taken by all concerned to ensure that neuroleptic medications are always used in a way that minimises the risks of problematic side-effects. One of the first principles of such a *"harm minimising"* approach involves developing a good understanding of the way that neuroleptic medication can sometimes contribute to producing "negative" symptoms.

What Do Neuroleptic Drugs Do?

The precise way in which neuroleptic drugs work is still not fully understood. Some reputable researchers have suggested that their major effect may involve inducing a feeling of "not getting worked up" or a "who cares" feeling.[73] In other words, they help by calming and relaxing a person who is feeling anxious, tense and generally "worked up" (remember that neuroleptic drugs are also sometimes called "major tranquillisers").

Professor Manfred Bleuler has suggested that these drugs may work by helping to *desensitise* a person whose problems originally stem from their excessive sensitivity (this was referred to earlier as "hypersensitivity"):

> Neuroleptics act by changing the activity or the sensitivity of definite neurological systems. The therapeutic consequence consists mainly in calming agitation and diminishing the sensitivity to stimulation both by psychodynamic [i.e. emotional] experience and by experience from the outer world. For these reasons, neuroleptics are of great value in many schizophrenic conditions.[74]

Very recently Professor Luc Ciompi has speculated on the possibility that neuroleptic drugs may have their *primary* impact on the emotional level, for example, by exerting a dampening action on certain parts of the limbic system.[75] *Such calming effects of medication may be very useful in helping a person to maintain their emotional stability during times of excessive stress and over-stimulation.* More specifically, they might help to break the psychotic "chain reaction" by reducing the amount of emotional energy which is available to drive it.

If these hypotheses are correct, it is easy to appreciate how the use of neuroleptic drugs might lead to problems if they were to have an excessive desensitising effect. Thus, whilst a *moderate* reduction of a person's sensitivity to stimulation, or the induction of a *mild* "who cares" feeling, might be very helpful at certain times, *too much* "desensitisation" could well contribute to a situation in which "negative" symptoms begin to predominate.[76] These comments describe such a situation of drug-induced "psychic indifference":

It is not uncommon to observe psychiatric patients who are lethargic, disinterested, asocial, or behaving oddly. Frequently, these symptoms are attributed to illness and not to medication. Yet, when dosages are reduced or drugs discontinued, a favourable transformation occurs in these patients. They become alert, talkative, sociable, show a broadening of interests, have more drive, and much of their odd behaviour vanishes. Clearly, these patients were "drugged" and much of their strange behaviour was medication-induced.[77]

"Invisible" Side-Effects

Some of the more common side-effects of neuroleptic medications, such as sedation (sleepiness), tremor (the "shakes"), and muscular stiffness, are usually easily recognised and often quite simple to treat. In addition to these, however, neuroleptic drugs can also produce a number of "invisible" side-effects which may not be readily obvious to an observer, nor easily identifiable as being due to prescribed medications. "Invisible" side-effects may include depression, loss of spontaneity, slowing of movement and thought, and dampening of creativity.[78] Some of these problems may be related to a *subtle* form of drug-induced Parkinson's disease which manifests in the form of emotional blunting, rather than as parkinsonism. As one standard psychiatric text advises:

> One should be alert to subtle parkinsonian-like symptoms because they can be confused with emotional withdrawal or retardation, and are readily treated by anti-parkinsonian medications. Indeed, one should not only watch for the conventional parkinsonian symptoms, such as mask-like [face] and shuffling gait, but also be aware that patients who appear apathetic, lacking in spontaneity, relatively unable to participate in social activities, lifeless, zombie-like, or drowsy, may be demonstrating subtle extrapyramidal side-effects.[79]

Although not everyone experiences such problems, for some people they can sometimes be quite severe. For example, one man gave the following graphic description of the effect that prescribed neuroleptic medications had on his inner life:

Four years ago I began having fortnightly injections . . . since then my periods of psychosis have stopped . . . Unfortunately, my personality has been so stifled that sometimes I think that the richness of my pre-injection days – even with brief outbursts of madness – is preferable to the numbed cabbage that I have become. I am advised by all doctors to continue with my injections and will do so, but in losing my periods of madness I have to pay with my soul, and the price of health seems twice as high as Everest. . . . [neuroleptic drugs] inhibit the imagination and, whereas once I lived in a fascinating ocean of imagination, I now exist in a mere puddle of it. I used to write poetry and prose because it released and satisfied something deep inside myself; now I find reading and writing an effort and my world inside is a desert.[80]

Fortunately, most people do not experience side-effects as severe as this. It is a fact, however, that many people *do* feel that their prescribed neuroleptic medications cause them serious problems. In a recent survey conducted by SANELINE, a mental health telephone help-line in Britain, many callers reported problems with medication side-effects. Some people described themselves as feeling like a "zombie" on medication; others said they felt they were separated from the outside world by a glass screen, that their senses were numbed, their willpower drained, and their lives meaningless. So common were these complaints that the author of the published report of the survey used the term "Neuroleptic-Induced Deficit Syndrome" to describe them.[81]

Zan Bockes has described similar experiences, which were made even worse by the guilt which was caused by her thinking that perhaps she was just being lazy:

Regular [neuroleptic] injections stabilised me enough to complete the semester, but those months seemed to drag on forever. Physically, I didn't feel too uncomfortable other than being stiff and "slowed down" most of the time, but what bothered me most was my inability to get interested in anything, to be curious about anything, or to feel any emotion about anything. I often wondered if [medication] was causing my profound lack of interest and energy, or if I was just being "lazy". I made efforts to exercise, to meet new people, to read new books, to write regularly in my journal – all to no avail. I spent most of my free time lying on my bed in my apartment.[82]

"Psychological" Side-Effects

Some physical side-effects of medications, such as tremor ("the shakes"), tardive dyskinesia, or weight gain may indirectly contribute to a person developing "negative" symptoms by causing social embarrassment and a subsequent desire to withdraw in order to avoid contact with other people. The stigma associated with the very fact of needing to take "psychiatric" medications – as opposed to medications for ordinary physical conditions – may in itself contribute to shame, guilt and embarrassment. Furthermore, the prospect of having to take these medications for the rest of their lives may have a significant demoralising effect on some people.

Side-Effects or "Negative" Symptoms?

Differentiating between "negative" symptoms and the side-effects of neuroleptic medication can be very difficult and expert assessment is required. In some cases, however, the person who is taking the drugs simply *knows* that they are causing problems, even though others may not necessarily agree with their opinion.

The following guidelines have been suggested as clues which may indicate that at least *some* of the person's problems are specifically related to the side-effects of their neuroleptic medication:[83]

- Persistent drowsiness (which is not related to lack of sleep).
- Reduction of "negative" symptoms if neuroleptic medication doses are reduced or neuroleptic medication is stopped altogether.
- Fewer "negative" symptoms on a different type of neuroleptic medication.
- *Rapid* improvement of "negative" symptoms on anti-parkinsonian "side-effect medication" such as Cogentin (benztropine), Kemadrin (procyclidine), or Artane (benzhexol).
- *Rapid* worsening of "negative" symptoms if side-effect medication is stopped.

As with the use of any therapeutic medications, a balance always has to be found between beneficial effects and undesired effects. In regard to schizophrenia, finding this balance is something of an art – both for the prescriber and the person taking the drugs – that requires patience and experience. Most importantly, the views of the person taking the medications should always be taken into account when anyone is attempting to decide which medications and dosages are most effective, and which dosage levels may be too high.[84]

(NOTE: Some specific guidelines for tailoring neuroleptic medications to achieve optimal benefits with minimal side-effects are described in Part Two of this book.)

"NEGATIVE" SYMPTOMS
AND THE BRAIN

As biological theories of schizophrenia have come to be heavily emphasised attempts have been made to explain "negative" symptoms *entirely* in terms of various kinds of brain abnormality. Well known authors such as Fuller Torrey, for example, have stated unequivocally that schizophrenia has been clearly proven to be a "brain disease", and that "negative" symptoms have been directly related to specific structural abnormalities of the brain.[85]

Despite the widespread popularity of such claims they remain controversial. Studies attempting to demonstrate that specific brain abnormalities are consistently associated with schizophrenia so far remain inconclusive, and *no reputable research has yet been able to show that there is a clear causal relationship between brain changes and "negative" symptoms.*[86] For example, even though evidence obtained from CT scan research is often said to have proven that schizophrenia is a "brain disease", the fact remains that the majority of people with a diagnosis of schizophrenia have *normal* CT scans.[87] Torrey himself acknowledges that only about 20% of people with schizophrenia have been shown to have abnormal brain scans.[88]

All other biological findings have also proven to be inconsistent, to vary over time, to be found in only small sub-groups of patients, or to be also present in people who do *not* have a diagnosis of schizophrenia – including some members of the so-called "normal" population!

Professor Luc Ciompi has suggested that if brain changes do occur – which may happen in a small minority of people – they could possibly be a *consequence* rather than a primary cause of social and emotional restriction and underactivity.[89] This view has received support from Dr. Timothy Crow, head of the Division of Psychiatry at the Clinical Research Centre of Northwick Park Hospital in London, which is regarded by some as one of the best schizophrenia research units in the world. Dr. Crow has said:

> The evidence is not yet decisive on the question of whether these structural [brain] changes precede or

are a consequence of [schizophrenia]. Some observations are consistent with the possibility that
sometimes they are precursors, but I predict that in
many cases they will prove to be sequelae [i.e.
consequences] of episodes of illness.[90]

At the present time it is impossible for anyone to answer the
complex "chicken and egg" question regarding what connection
there might be between brain changes and the "negative"
symptoms of schizophrenia. Furthermore, even if some
abnormalities *do* exist in the structure and function of a
particular person's brain, scientists are still unable to say precisely
what effects this might have on the person's behaviour and ability
to function.

In this regard it is worth reflecting on the observations made
by the renowned neurologist, Dr. Oliver Sacks. In his book,
"Awakenings" (which was recently made into a popular
Hollywood film), Dr. Sacks described his experiences in treating
the last survivors of the great sleeping-sickness epidemic which
swept the world in the 1920s. Though some of these people had
been lost in extremely severe states of regression for over forty
years, Dr. Sacks was struck by the lack of consistency between their
clinical state and the condition of their brains:

> There was, moreover, a rather poor correlation
> between the severity of the clinical picture and that of
> the pathological picture, in so far as the latter could be
> judged by microscopic or chemical means: one saw
> profoundly disabled patients with remarkably few signs
> of disease in the brain, and one saw evidences of
> widespread tissue-destruction in patients who were
> scarcely disabled at all.[91]

These observations convinced Dr. Sacks that it was the *whole*
person – not just the state of their brain – together with their *total*
circumstances, which would determine what happened to them
in the long-term:

> What was clear, from these discrepancies, was that
> there were many other determinants of clinical state
> and behaviour besides localised changes in the brain
> ... It seemed ... as if the "quality" of the individual –

his "strengths" and "weaknesses", resistances and
pliancies, motives and experiences, etc. – played a large
part in determining the severity, course, and form of
his illness.[91]

The wisdom of attempting to explain the existence of
"negative" symptoms entirely in terms of brain abnormalities has
been questioned by a number of internationally regarded
authorities on schizophrenia. For example, Professor Strauss and
his colleagues – in keeping with their holistic approach – have
argued that psychological and social factors must always be taken
into account as well.[92]

Our growing understanding of how the brain works has
recently raised the possibility that the actual physical structure of
a person's brain might change in accordance with the amount of
environmental stimulation they receive – a phenomenon known
as "neuronal plasticity".[93] Some researchers using CT scans to
study the brain have speculated on the possibility that prolonged
exposure to stress might lead to deteriorative changes in the
brain ("pseudo-atrophy") which may, in some cases, be reversible
(i.e. not permanent).[94] These observations suggest that *the human
brain may have a far greater potential for adaptive change than has
previously been thought possible.*

In light of these exciting possibilities it is sad to think that an
uncritical acceptance of the as yet unproven claims regarding the
existence of serious brain abnormalities in people with a
diagnosis of schizophrenia may be contributing in a tangible way
to the on-going demoralisation of patients, relatives, and mental
health professionals alike. This situation is even more poignant
when it is realised that such demoralisation may itself be one of
the most powerful factors contributing to the development of
"negative" symptoms!

Until such time as *all* the facts are known it is good to keep an
open mind. In any case, the observation that some people with a
diagnosis of schizophrenia have been known to recover even after
many years of withdrawal and apathy[95] must seriously challenge
the idea that any kind of permanent and irreversible brain
deterioration could possibly be *solely* responsible for causing all
"negative" symptoms.

THE "VICIOUS CIRCLE" OF "NEGATIVE" SYMPTOMS

Social withdrawal, emotional "shut-down", and post-psychotic "retreat" may begin as a vulnerable person's attempts to reduce their exposure to stress, over-stimulation, and emotional pain. If used in a *selective* way as a *temporary* means of self-protection, these strategies can be quite effective and, as Professor Strauss has pointed out, they may even help a person with schizophrenia to survive some of their difficult ordeals.[96]

Even the most useful coping strategies can sometimes be used excessively, however, and if they are, problems may result. For example, a highly sensitive person who uses withdrawal to prevent him or herself from becoming over-stimulated might go too far and thus end up receiving *too little* stimulation. Finding the ideal balance between over-stimulation and under-stimulation can sometimes be a problem in itself, as Elizabeth Farr's experience illustrates:

> Not moving came naturally. It was the way things had to be. It was almost as if this were a compensation to help de-stimulate me, like a way to subtract the lack of physical movement from the excessive sensory stimulation I experienced. *It was always hard to find the right balance of stimulation.* Sensory over-stimulation was disturbing to my precarious mental balance, but just as devastating was relative sensory deprivation. I lived alone, which was desirable to the extent that I could control my environment enough to be able to retire into the privacy of my own apartment when I was feeling over-stimulated. But then I tended to get too isolated; my apartment became like a sensory deprivation chamber. When I was away from human contact for long periods of time I began to drift from reality.[97]

Compared with the stresses and anxiety of over-stimulation a state of relative emotional and sensory under-stimulation may provide a person with a very welcome sanctuary at times. For example, when used for a limited time by a person who is struggling with a very difficult situation (such as during the highly vulnerable period immediately following a psychotic episode), even a relatively *extreme* degree of withdrawal, avoidance and "shut-down" may provide a desperately needed "cocoon" of safety in which undisturbed rest is possible for at least a little while.

For some people, however, self-protective withdrawal and "shut-down" can begin to develop into habitual – perhaps virtually automatic – responses to perceived threat and discomfort. If such coping responses do start to become deeply ingrained habits, what was once very helpful to a person may begin to work against them. Instead of being a useful *temporary* coping mechanism, withdrawal and avoidance may start to become a way of life.

Anyone who remains under-stimulated for too long may eventually experience an *increase* in such "negative" symptoms as apathy, slowness, and lack of initiative. This can happen because everyone needs a certain minimum level of stimulation in order to maintain their ability to function adequately.[98] (Remember that under-stimulation has been identified as one of the main factors contributing to "institutionalisation".) In some cases the psychological effects of prolonged social under-stimulation may be further added to by the side-effects of prescribed medications, demoralisation, and some of the other influences described earlier.

"Negative" symptoms can tend to become self-perpetuating because anyone who finds themselves cut off from the ordinary activities of daily life for too long may begin to lose both their self-confidence and their basic skills of living. After all, the saying "If you don't use it, you lose it" applies just as much to the skills needed for socialising, self-care and employment as it does to physical abilities such as sporting skills and physical fitness. Confidence and life skills can usually be re-gained, but only when a person gradually begins doing things again – which is often the very last thing they feel motivated to do or capable of.

As a result of these combined effects some people can eventually begin to find themselves being drawn into a kind of "vicious circle" of "negative" symptoms which can be difficult for them to break out of. One person gave the following description of his own experience of this:

Avoidance can go too far. In my behaviour this was
manifest, for example, by not getting up before
10 o'clock, going to bed early, not going to parties or
pubs, and not mixing with my friends. I developed a
total negativism toward other people. The reason in my
case was that I felt inadequate. . . . I would stand in a
group of people and not take part at all. I wanted to
contribute but could not do so. . . . Much social
withdrawal, in my experience, is a reaction to one's
own inadequacies. Sometimes the feeling is so great
that one *must* be alone. Withdrawal is then protective
but it cannot last forever. . . . Everyone needs to keep
mentally occupied and this is especially true of people
with schizophrenia. . . . If my periods of convalescence
are too long I tend to get lazy and become
unmotivated. . . . I believe that quite a few people with
schizophrenia drop out completely because the apathy
takes a complete hold.[99]

Many people who have started to feel apathetic and unmotivated begin to feel guilty about themselves because deep down
they do not want to be this way. If feelings of guilt and self-blame
become too severe, however, they can make it even *more* difficult
for the person to change their behaviour. Such feelings may
paralyse action by convincing a person that nothing they do will
ever work anyway so why should they even bother trying. Being
angrily accused of laziness, irresponsibility or unfriendliness by
others who do not really understand the true nature of the
situation sometimes adds even further to an already heavy burden
of guilt. In addition, a person who remains inactive and
unmotivated for a long time may begin to lose touch with their
friends and acquaintances as these people gradually begin to lose
interest and start drifting away.

It is not difficult to imagine how anyone finding themselves in
this kind of situation may soon begin to lose any sense of hope for
the future. As their feelings of demoralisation grow some people
experience an increasing temptation to cease struggling against
the tide which seems to be pulling them away from the world of
living. Sadly, some people may begin to succumb to the twin
temptations of laziness and irresponsibility and simply "let

themselves go". For others, abuse of drugs – whether social, illicit or prescribed – may promise a temporary escape into oblivion or a short-lived experience of a more highly energised state. What often motivates these potentially self-destructive behaviours is the craving for relief from a pervasive and painful state of *boredom*:

> Much of a patient's actions of self-abuse or transgressions against others may stem from a painful "boredom". In a recent study, when patients recovering from psychosis in the community were interviewed about their lives, "their principal complaint was of boredom – rated by them as much more problematic than psychotic symptoms", and the high prevalence of their using stimulants and mind-altering drugs and sleeping excessively is a consequence of what they feel to be empty and uninteresting lives. This boredom is magnified by anti-psychotic medications, even when they are taken in just slightly more than the minimal dosage.[100]

Eventually, anyone who has remained under-stimulated for a long period of time may have become so used to their state of social isolation and emotional detachment that *they may begin to resist attempts to alter it*. In extreme cases the person's strong dislike of any kind of change may result in hostility towards anyone who is felt to be intruding with unwanted demands.[101] This may occur even when attempts to stimulate change are made by people motivated by genuine concern for the person's welfare. In time, helpers who are constantly met with hostility or on-going resistance may eventually become worn-out and gradually begin reducing their investment of time and effort in trying to change the situation.

At this point yet another influence may contribute to shaping a person's fate. This occurs when people who have been providing valuable support and encouragement start to believe that perhaps there really is no point in hoping for any change in the situation since there are no obvious reasons to believe that it is possible or likely. Such pessimistic beliefs, *even if they are never openly stated*, can have a powerful influence on a person who has a high level of "negative" symptoms. Professor Luc Ciompi has found that a person's own expectations about their future,

together with those of their family and others who are closely
involved – such as mental health professionals – seem often to act
as *self-fulfilling prophecies.*[102] In other words, when people expect
that no improvement is possible, it actually becomes more likely
that this is precisely what will happen.

Ironically, the widely held belief that "negative" symptoms are
both permanent and untreatable may itself contribute to the
creation of pessimistic self-fulfilling prophecies by eroding the
hopes and expectations of *everyone* concerned. For example, the
use by some mental health professionals of terms such as "deficit
state" in reference to people who are considered to have primary
"negative" symptoms[103] seems to imply a belief that such people
have reached a state in which they no longer have any potential
or capacity to change:

> "Deficit" connotes a degree of finality and irreversibility
> and pessimism and may, in fact, be misleading when
> applied in particular to the negative symptoms
> expressed by the schizophrenic patient. Such a term
> suggests that the patient is mentally dead or incom-
> petent. This is a damaging notion when it dominates
> the thinking of anyone working with an individual with
> schizophrenia, for it treats the patient as merely the
> unfortunate recipient of some dread malady and avoids
> the possibility of identifying areas of struggle within the
> patient regarding these very issues . . .[104]

"NEGATIVE" SYMPTOMS
IN THE LONG-TERM

To one degree or another many people who have a high level of "negative" symptoms seem to have become stuck in the "vicious circle" which these very "negative" symptoms have helped to create. In such cases, outward appearances may tend to reinforce the impression that there is very little real hope that escape from this dilemma is possible. Despite the great difficulties that are involved and the very real challenges that must be faced, however, there is a good deal of evidence to show that many people are eventually able to move beyond this predicament, and that many will go on to regain capacities they had apparently lost forever.

Over the years it has often been noted that people who have a diagnosis of "chronic schizophrenia" sometimes respond in a quite unexpected way to changes in their environment. For example, there have been many reports of incidents in which even very withdrawn, apathetic individuals have suddenly "come out of their shells" to take on a leading role in rescue operations during emergency situations such as a fire or a flood.[105] In addition to such apparently spontaneous occurrences researchers have found that people who are involved in active psychosocial rehabilitation programmes often begin to show significantly fewer "negative" symptoms such as social withdrawal, flatness of affect, poverty of speech, general slowness, and underactivity.[106] A range of psychosocial strategies have now been shown to be quite effective in reducing some "negative" symptoms. These strategies include:

- client education programmes.[107]
- initiatives which foster positive and supportive communication within families.[108]
- certain types of skilfully conducted psychotherapy.[109]

Though no one is yet able to fully account for the effectiveness of these strategies, the very fact that they frequently do help lends considerable support to the view that *"negative" symptoms are often much less fixed and untreatable than they are usually said to be.* In keeping with this view, a growing number of highly regarded authorities now question the idea that only "positive" symptoms are treatable. Their beliefs are supported by several long-term studies which have shown that even people who have lived with schizophrenia for many years may still eventually experience substantial improvements in their condition.

Professor Courtenay Harding and her colleagues, as a result of their research into the causes of "chronicity", have challenged the belief that a person who has had "negative" symptoms for a long time is unlikely to improve. In fact, they concluded, people with typical "negative" symptoms at one point in time can sometimes go on to significantly improve or recover even after decades of "chronicity".[110] Similar opinions have been expressed by Professor Manfred Bleuler, whose life-long studies led him to the firm conclusion that such "late" improvements are not only possible, but that they are in fact actually more likely to occur than any continuing process of deterioration directly related to schizophrenia. Professor Bleuler has summarised his considered beliefs thus:

> Generations of psychiatrists felt that schizophrenia was a process psychosis always progressing to complete deterioration ... and that this final state could only progress or remain unchanged, but never improve. I am certain today that the contrary is true. More than 20 or 30 years after the onset of a severe schizophrenic psychosis the general tendencies are towards an improvement. This improvement ... consists of a real reappearance of both healthy intellectual life and very warm-hearted, very human emotional life in certain situations and in contact with certain persons.[111]

Professor Bleuler saw that symptoms of any kind were only one level of a person's personality. Beneath them, he felt, much of the person's inner life always remains human, natural and healthy. Indeed, even people who have had the most severe and long-standing disturbances always maintain "a warm and human heart", though it may be obscured by their outward behaviour. Such people, says Professor Bleuler:

> always show signs of normal psychological life existing behind their psychotic behaviour. ... the ability to

reason and to think logically is never lost, but goes on
at the same time as the illogical and chaotic inner life
continues. . . . I was also interested to observe and to
provoke human feelings, very fine emotions, signs of a
sound and touching affect in [people living with
schizophrenia] who were formerly considered to be
burnt-out, petrified, without human emotions.[112]

Professor Ciompi has also found that people with a high level
of "negative" symptoms sometimes improve "to an astonishing
degree" even after decades of hospitalisation when they are
provided with a safe and supportive therapeutic environment.[113]
These facts suggest that even the most apparently "chronic"
person should never be thought of as being like an extinct
volcano (a comparison reflected in expressions such as "burnt-
out chronic schizophrenic", which were once quite commonly
used). Many such people, it seems, are perhaps more aptly
compared to *dormant* volcanoes which still retain the capacity to
come to life.

In the light of all of these findings, Professor Ciompi believes
that "negative" symptoms cannot – and should not – be
considered as necessarily irreversible in the long-term.[114]

**In the next section a wide range of practical strategies are
described which may help to prevent a person from developing
"negative" symptoms, or which may help to alleviate the severity
of any "negative" symptoms which a person has already
developed.**

Part Two

Preventing and Alleviating "Negative" Symptoms

PRACTICAL STRATEGIES FOR PREVENTING AND ALLEVIATING "NEGATIVE" SYMPTOMS

As was explained in Part One, many factors might contribute in some way to causing a person to develop "negative" symptoms. In most cases a number of different factors acting together over a period of time (possibly quite a long time) will have led to the gradual wearing down of a person's energy, self-confidence, abilities, morale and hope. Once this has happened the "vicious circle" of "negative" symptoms may have then begun the process of locking the demoralised person into a self-perpetuating state of isolation and inactivity which has become difficult for them to break out of without help.

In some quarters the view has arisen that there is really very little that can be done to help a person who is in this state. Such views often fail to appreciate the highly complex nature of these problems, and the fact that *in the vast majority of cases there will be at least* **some** *social and psychological factors contributing to the development and persistence of "negative" symptoms which can either be prevented or at least minimised.*

Since every person's situation is entirely unique *no one* can possibly predict in advance what may or may not help someone who has these problems. Furthermore, the very fact that many people with a diagnosis of schizophrenia *do* improve considerably over time shows that it is never wise to prematurely give up on any particular person. If there is a golden rule for people struggling with "negative" symptoms – whether they are receiving help or providing it – it is to constantly strive to remain focused as much as possible on the *positive*!

Anyone who feels it may be worthwhile attempting to tackle these problems must be willing to experiment. In other words, they must be prepared to try different things in order to discover for themselves whether or not some of them might lead to positive changes. Keeping an open mind and always allowing room for the *possibility* of growth and change will help to create the right attitude and spirit for such experimentation. Furthermore, real progress will be much more likely if attention is constantly directed toward the *whole person and their total situation* rather than simply toward "symptoms" or "illness".

In many cases a "team effort" which involves the person with "negative" symptoms, his or her relatives, friends, and mental health professionals all working together towards a common goal, will achieve the best results. Above all, patience is required by everyone concerned because change, when it does occur, often comes very slowly and very gradually. Helpers should always try to remember that very real emotional pain caused some people to withdraw and go into a "shut-down" state in the first place. Remembering this can help to reduce any tendency to become impatient or to badger during times when progress may seem too slow.

Since schizophrenia generally, and "negative" symptoms in particular, are both the end product of *many* different influences, both may respond in time to quite simple and practical strategies, such as the ones described below. Virtually all of the recommendations made in the following pages are quite *simple*, in the sense that they require no special equipment or training. Sensitivity, compassion and basic common sense are all that are needed. "Simple" does not necessarily mean "easy", however, and it is to be expected that real effort, tolerance, patience and persistence will be required in abundance of everyone concerned.

The particular combination of strategies that may prove to be most effective in any given case will depend to a large extent on each person's individual needs, abilities and specific circumstances. In the beginning it is often best to select one or two strategies to work with rather than attempting to change too many things at once. Remember that any particular strategy should be persisted with for a reasonable period of time because it can often take a while before any tangible changes start to become obvious.

The specific strategies which are described in detail in this section include the following:

1   Understand the Nature and Causes of "Negative" Symptoms p.63.
2   Cultivate Hope and Positive Attitudes p.64.
3   Create a Safe Environment p.65.
4   Create a Safe and Supportive Family Atmosphere p.67.
5   Learn to Appreciate Silence p.71.

6   Use Neuroleptic Medications Wisely p.72.
7   Work For Recovery p.78.
8   Gradually Increase Activity and Responsibility p.81.
9   Maintain a Structured Routine of Activity p.81.
10 Find a Balanced Level of Stimulation p.83.
11 Cultivate Patience and Persistence p.84.
12 Practise Gentleness p.85.
13 Adopt a Healthy Lifestyle p.86.
14 Utilise Counselling or Psychotherapy p.87.
15 Learn Effective Coping Skills p.88.
16 Cultivate Self-Esteem p.91.
17 Find a Meaning and Purpose in Life p.93.
18 Confront New Situations and Responsibilities p.95.
19 Beware of Depression p.96.
20 Guard Against the "Seduction of Madness" p.98.
21 Respect and Nurture Spirituality p.100.

(1) *Understand the Nature and Causes of "Negative" Symptoms*

Before anyone can deal effectively with "negative" symptoms it is necessary that they begin to develop some understanding of how and why these particular problems occur. Usually a number of interacting psychological, social, spiritual and physical factors are involved. For example, social withdrawal and emotional "shut-down" often serve the vital purpose of protecting a hypersensitive person from stress and over-stimulation; post-psychotic "retreat" may be a transitory phase which is necessary for recuperation and healing to occur; "positive withdrawal" may be a long-standing personality characteristic which allows a highly sensitive person to live at a safely comfortable distance from others.

Though such "negative" symptoms can all be useful, they sometimes lead into a "vicious circle" which can eventually become a painful trap. Demoralisation, which is a common problem for many people with a diagnosis of schizophrenia, often plays a very significant part in the onset of "negative" symptoms. If it becomes severe, demoralisation may sometimes lead into depression. In some cases the effects of prolonged institutional-isation, the side-effects of prescribed medications, and Post-Traumatic Stress Disorder (PTSD) are also significant.

In addition to these *secondary* symptoms it is possible that *some* people also experience "negative" symptoms which are somehow more directly related to schizophrenia itself (i.e. *primary* "negative" symptoms). Since primary and secondary "negative" symptoms cannot readily be distinguished the American Psychiatric Association recommends that every effort should be made to deal with the various factors that may be contributing to the persistence of secondary "negative" symptoms before a person is presumed to have primary "negative" symptoms.[115] Some authorities have suggested that "negative" symptoms should not be considered as primary unless a person has had such symptoms persistently for at least one year in the *absence* of the various possible causative factors that were described in Part One.[116]

(2) *Cultivate Hope and Positive Attitudes*

In the long run some people are probably more disabled by their feelings of hopelessness and despair than they are by schizophrenia or "negative" symptoms. Hopefulness and positive attitudes are so vital to mental health and well-being, in fact, that some people who have recovered from the worst of their ordeals have said that a state of hopelessness is itself the *real* "illness"![117]

There is little doubt that the "vicious circle" of "negative" symptoms is often created when a person who has started to become demoralised begins to believe that there really is no hope for them, and nothing at all they can do to improve their life. The dogma that there is little that can be done to alleviate "negative" symptoms often only helps to confirm such despair.

Recent research has quite clearly shown that many people who have a diagnosis of schizophrenia *will* go on to significantly improve or recover completely, and that progressive deterioration over time is *not* an inevitable occurrence. Even if "negative" symptoms have been severe and prolonged late improvements may still occur. Sometimes even the most severe "negative" symptoms are *transitory* (during a period of post-psychotic "retreat", for example) and will gradually diminish over time without any specific treatment. These facts suggest that within everyone there may exist untapped healing powers together with an ever-present potential for growth and change.

Research conducted by Professor Ciompi and others has clearly shown that self-fulfilling prophecies are an important factor in schizophrenia and that people's expectations about their future often seem to have a significant influence on what will actually happen.. Cultivating and maintaining positive attitudes and expectations, and clinging to realistic hopefulness, are therefore extremely important.

Hope always empowers and energises people. Anyone who feels hopeful about themselves and the possibility of having a better quality of life will be energised by their hope to actively seek ways of improving their situation. For many people the turning point out of "stuckness" and despair comes with the re-awakening of hope, as Patricia Deegan has explained:

> For months I sat and smoked cigarettes until it was time to collapse back into a drugged and dreamless sleep. But one day something changed ... A tiny, fragile spark of hope appeared and promised that there could be something more than all of this darkness. ... All of the polemic and technology of psychiatry, psychology, social work, and science cannot account for this phenomenon of hope. But those of us who have recovered know that this grace is real. We lived it. It is our shared secret.[118]

(3) *Create a Safe Environment*

Some "negative" symptoms can be seen as extreme coping strategies which hypersensitive people use in order to protect themselves from overwhelming threat. Social withdrawal and "emotional shut-down", in particular, can be viewed as providing a vulnerable person with a "safety shield" against over-stimulation, and a "very necessary protective shell" against emotional pain.

It is likely that a person's need to use these extreme means of self-protection can be reduced considerably – and possibly even made unnecessary – if they are able to find an environment in which they feel safe. It is worth remembering that originally the term "asylum" referred to a sanctuary and a place of refuge. The original intention in creating such places was to provide an environment in which vulnerable and emotionally distressed people would at last be enabled to feel safe and secure.

On the basis of his extensive research Professor Luc Ciompi has concluded that the most basic therapeutic principles for people with a diagnosis of schizophrenia correspond to ancient common sense wisdom. Thus, Professor Ciompi says:

> More than anything else [such people] are confused, anxious, hypersensitive, and vulnerable people; therefore, anything contributing to a relaxed, simple, clearly defined environment will have a beneficial effect on the intricate pattern of their thoughts and emotions. Such an approach makes sense not only to the medical specialists but also – and this is far more important in everyday life – to the nursing staff as well as to family members, employers, and lay helpers.[119]

In Professor Manfred Bleuler's view the basic guiding principles of good psychosocial care are these:

> The [person] is in need of steady and clear human relations, just as close and as distant as is suitable for him and the situation; he is in need of surroundings which enable and stimulate him to be active in accordance with his strength, ability and interests, alternating with rest and relaxation. He also needs both relief from social responsibilities and confrontation with responsibilities, each adapted to his actual needs and the situation.[120]

For anyone working to create an environment of safety, Professor Bleuler has especially emphasised the following points:[121]

- Quiet and orderly surroundings, as well as regularity in the day's schedule, have a beneficial calming influence on people.
- The calm and benevolent attitudes and behaviour of others (such as helpers and relatives) is invaluable.
- Tranquillity can be fostered in a number of ways, including: "talking and togetherness" (which is especially important); skilfully conducted psychotherapy; the use of neuroleptic medications (if and when they are indicated).

When attempting to provide a safe, low-stress environment it is important to remember that hypersensitive individuals may be aware of, and adversely effected by, stimuli which other people might barely notice. For example, some people may find the noise of a radio or TV program in the background, or the overheard sounds of other people talking, to be extremely distracting and confusing at times. In addition, many people with a diagnosis of schizophrenia seem to be extremely sensitive to subtle non-verbal communications or to the "hidden" messages in the speech and gestures of others (e.g. being able to pick up what other people *really* feel, as opposed to what they may be only pretending to feel). An illustration of this is provided by a woman who has described how she carefully scrutinised her therapist's behaviour in order to reassure herself that his caring and concern for her was genuine and not simply a pretence designed to lull her into a false sense of trust. She said:

> At the start, I didn't listen to what you said most of the time but I watched like a hawk for your expression and the sound of your voice. . . . I would add all this up to see if it seemed to show love. The words were nothing compared to the feelings you showed. I sensed that you felt confident I could be helped and that there was hope for the future. It's like talking to a frightened horse or dog. They may not know your words but the calm and strength and confidence that you convey helps them to feel safe again.[122]

Because of their sensitivity, any measures which help to simplify the environment and which reduce the amount of complex, confusing or ambiguous stimulation the person must cope with are likely to be extremely beneficial. Furthermore, helpers who provide *non-intrusive* emotional support and sensitively timed personal contact can help to foster in a recovering person an ongoing feeling of safety without the risk of restricting the natural unfolding of their abilities.

(4) *Create a Safe and Supportive Family Atmosphere*
An ideal family environment is one which is safe, supportive, tolerant and accepting. Real families are never like this all the time, of course – people are only human, after all! Furthermore, the presence of a person with a diagnosis of schizophrenia can place

extraordinary demands on *every* member of a family. High levels of "negative" symptoms, in particular, can severely test everyone's tolerance, patience and love. This is especially likely if members of the family have little real understanding of schizophrenia and the specific needs of a person with "negative" symptoms.

Because family members often find these particular symptoms especially difficult to deal with, the person with them can easily become the focus of criticism and conflict. Unfortunately this may eventually contribute to making matters even worse. On the other hand, research has shown that positive and supportive communications within the family can actually help to reduce some "negative" symptoms, such as a person's continued need for self-protective "shut down" and social withdrawal.[123]

On the basis of her own experience Esso Leete has made a number of specific suggestions which may be useful to families who are attempting to deal constructively with these problems.[124] Though these guidelines may often be frustratingly difficult to adhere to in the real world of day to day living, they may at least provide family members with a basic framework upon which to build as they work to develop and refine their own particular methods of coping.

(a) *Try to be non-judgemental*

Relatives should aim to avoid making critical, disparaging or hostile comments as much as possible. It is better to express any dissatisfaction in as emotionally neutral a manner as possible. If criticism is necessary, it should be constructive and made in a spirit of love and understanding.

(b) *Avoid being arbitrary*

Variable, inconsistent and unpredictable responses by family members to problematic behaviours are a significant cause of stress for many people living with schizophrenia. This can be reduced by: clarifying all expectations; sticking to previously agreed plans or promises; setting and consistently enforcing limits; explaining any unexpected changes of plans or routines as simply and clearly as possible.

(c) *Treat what the person says seriously*

People with a diagnosis of schizophrenia may begin to feel worthless and cut off from others if their personal opinions and beliefs – especially those that may be different or unusual – are routinely and automatically treated as merely a nonsensical "part of their illness". In order to avoid this, family members should try to remain tolerant to differences of opinion and belief:

> It is fine to disagree or to clarify your point of view, but please do not discount our thoughts or feelings. Indeed, let us ventilate them. Consider that we may have a different perspective, not that we are simply delusional or psychotic. Take what we say seriously. Do not be condescending. Realise that many times we accomplish reality testing with our remarks to you, and we need the assurance of your calm, caring, logical feedback.[125]

(d) *Communicate clearly and concisely*

Hypersensitive individuals who are susceptible to being overwhelmed by excessive or confusing stimulation can be helped by relatives who communicate clearly and concisely. This can be done by trying to minimise distractions during any conversation; speaking slowly and clearly; providing information in small amounts (e.g. short, simple sentences); avoiding ambiguous communications (i.e. those which may have more than one possible meaning or interpretation); always allowing the person adequate time to respond to questions or requests.

(e) *Provide constant support and encouragement*

People with "negative" symptoms should receive constant encouragement to do as much as they are able to. At first this may only involve very small and simple tasks (such as household chores, personal hygiene and grooming, short conversations). Whilst it is vital not to have unrealistically high expectations of the person it is also very important not to have *too few* expectations of them! It is better to encourage someone to do things by giving them praise and rewarding their efforts than it is to punish or criticise them for not doing things. Giving a person honest, constructive feedback which focuses on their strengths helps them to know how they are doing and what is expected of them. They should also be asked for their views and feelings about any family matters which are relevant to them. Esso Leete says:

Do not smother with control or constant suggestions;
encourage us to do all we can. Build on small successes.
Have and demonstrate confidence in us and our
abilities, but encourage us to ask for help whenever
necessary. Find a role for us in the family other than
being the "sick" member. Focus on our strengths. Do not
"institutionalise" us at home. Foster a sense of indepen-
dence, and rescue only in a real emergency. Provide a
family atmosphere that supports improvement . . . and
accepts us, no matter what.[125]

(f) *Respect the person's need for emotional distance*

Family members who are able to understand the person's need to
create a space for personal "time out" as a way to avoid becoming
emotionally over-stimulated are likely to feel more tolerant and
accepting of it. They will not take it as a personal rejection. This
will inevitably help to prevent a "vicious circle" of escalating
criticism and *mutual* withdrawal from beginning. Esso Leete has
explained that being able to create an emotional distance from
others may be crucial at times:

> Accept that many times we have a real need for seclusion
> and withdrawal from our environment. I have found it
> an invaluable means of getting the distance I need from
> something that was becoming overwhelming. Do not
> take our withdrawal from you personally. A private place
> (a bedroom, for example) may be our sanctuary from
> stress. This "time out" can be used constructively to cope
> with our symptoms.[126]

Family members may also find it useful to pay close attention
to whether the person's "negative" symptom behaviours tend to
increase or decrease in response to events that may be affecting
their emotional state. For example, does the person tend to
become more withdrawn, uncommunicative, and generally more
"unreachable" in response to any of the following:

- intense displays of emotion in the family (e.g. arguments, celebrations);
- excessive pressure to perform (e.g. feeling "pushed");
- experiences of "failure" (e.g. attempting things and giving up);

- achievement of success by siblings (e.g. brothers or sisters leaving home, gaining employment or promotion, graduation, marriage, etc.).

On the other hand there may be certain occurrences which seem to lead to a decrease in "negative" symptoms. For example, the person might be observed to be less withdrawn, more communicative, and generally more "animated" following:

- positive, personally rewarding experiences (e.g. finding a job, starting a new relationship, successfully completing an important task);
- developing new interests and activities outside the family home;
- improvement in a previously tense emotional atmosphere in the home;
- resolution of specific conflicts with family members (e.g. more harmonious relationships developed with siblings, parents, spouse).

The question of how much to "push" someone who is presently unmotivated and lacking in drive is one that troubles many families. Since every person and every family situation is different and unique, however, there can be no hard and fast rules about this issue. *Finding the right balance between too much pressure and too little is ultimately an art that only experience can teach.* Whilst struggling to find this balance it should never be forgotten that *every* member of the family has both rights and responsibilities. Everyone, including the person with "negative" symptoms, must assume responsibility for their own role in the family and for working within the limits of their abilities to improve their situation. Although people living with schizophrenia need everyone's support and encouragement in abundance, they should never be given it to such an extent that they become mere passive recipients of care with no responsibilities of their own.

(5) *Learn to Appreciate Silence*
People with "negative" symptoms sometimes feel pressured to speak or to engage in conversation with well-meaning friends or acquaintances. Such pressure may have the opposite effect to the one intended, however, since it can cause a person who lacks self-

confidence and self-esteem to feel anxious, which may then lead them into further "shut-down" and withdrawal. This dilemma can be avoided by developing an appreciation of the value of spending time with someone without the need to speak.

The old saying that "silence is golden" is a reminder of an often forgotten fact. Sharing *non-verbal* activities such as walking, listening to music, watching TV, reading, gardening, or craft-work – or even just being together without doing anything in particular – can help to reduce the pressure on a quiet, withdrawn person, whilst still allowing an opportunity for them to gradually develop trust. Just sitting quietly with a very withdrawn and emotionally unexpressive person can be a way of communicating caring and concern for them in a non-pressuring way. (Not bothering to spend time with an uncommunicative person may, on the other hand, tend to make them feel rejected, inadequate and worthless.)

At certain times many people with "negative" symptoms may find it easier to express their feelings and thoughts in non-verbal ways, such as through art, writing, music, and so on. Domestic pets can provide a completely non-threatening form of companionship and may even become important "friends" to people with low self-esteem and limited social confidence.

Many people with a diagnosis of schizophrenia can and do enjoy social contact with others as long as they do not feel too much pressure to interact or speak. The following example highlights this fact:

> [Some] patients like to be with other people as long as they do not have to interact with them directly. One such patient, for instance, enjoyed going to family parties as long as he could sit slightly apart and was not expected to speak to anyone. Another had said he liked to go and visit his aunt. His aunt was surprised to hear this as during these visits he would just sit in a chair and say nothing.[127]

(6) *Use Neuroleptic Medications Wisely*

It is an unfortunate fact that the neuroleptic drugs which are the mainstay of the usual medical treatment of schizophrenia often have side-effects which contribute to "negative" symptoms (many of these effects were described in Part One). For some people, these side-effects become much more than a mere inconvenience or minor irritation. In fact the potential effectiveness of many of the numerous practical strategies which are outlined in this book may never be fully realised if a person's level of energy and motivation are constantly restricted by the unwanted effects of their prescribed medication. Consequently, *it is absolutely vital that these medications be used in a sensitive and intelligent way in order to eliminate side-effects, or at least minimise them as much as possible.*

The first and most important principle to remember in achieving optimal benefits from neuroleptic medication is to always respect the unique individuality of the person receiving treatment. Since every human being is different, each person's need for, and response to, neuroleptic drugs is bound to be different. Because there are very few "hard and fast" rules regarding the use of these drugs, experimentation over a period of time is really the only reliable way to discover what seems to work best.[128] *The ideal drug regime for any given individual can only be determined on a trial-and-error basis.* The following principles should guide the rational use of neuroleptic medication:

(A) *THOROUGH ASSESSMENT*

  (i) Any person who has significant "negative" symptoms should have their current medication regime carefully reviewed by a competent mental health professional in order to determine whether or not the side-effects of these drugs might be contributing to their problems.

 (ii) Anyone who has been on high doses of medication for a long time, or who is taking a combination of several different drugs, should be carefully assessed to determine whether or not they have a genuine continuing need for these medications.

(iii) It is very important to be aware of the fact that the relative proportions of "positive" and "negative" symptoms that a person has will often change over time. During the first few years following diagnosis many people mainly experience "positive" psychotic symptoms such as delusions and hallucinations. (It is usually these particular symptoms which have led to the diagnosis being made in the first place.) Over time there is often a tendency for these "positive" symptoms to become less prominent and for the "negative" type symptoms to become the major concern (some of the reasons for this were outlined in Part One). Since neuroleptic medications are generally most clearly of benefit in controlling "positive" symptoms, it is likely that for some people continuing on high doses of medication over long periods may eventually begin to have more disadvantages than benefits.[129]

On the basis of his own extensive clinical experience and research Professor Manfred Bleuler concluded that neuroleptic medication may be useful during psychotic episodes as well as in helping a person to maintain their emotional stability over longer periods. In the long-term, however, he felt that continuous medication is only warranted if experience has *proven* that "relapse" inevitably occurs without it.[130] At the present time it is impossible to predict in advance who may be at greater risk of experiencing "relapse" without medication and who may not be. Some researchers have estimated that up to 50% of people on long-term "maintenance" medication for schizophrenia might *not* be any worse off if their medication was gradually ceased.[131]

(B) *EXPERIMENTATION*

Quite often the only reliable way to determine if a person's "negative" symptoms are related to medication side-effects is for the person's medication regime to be changed in some way and then to observe what happens.[132] Treatment options can include one or more of the following:

- reducing the total dosage of neuroleptic medication;
- switching to a different neuroleptic drug which may have fewer side-effects;
- using antiparkinsonian medications ("side effect tablets") such as Cogentin (benztropine), Kemadrin (procyclidine) or Artane (benzhexol).

If any of these measures result in rapid and significant improvement it is reasonable to assume that neuroleptic medication side-effects were indeed contributing to the person's "negative" symptoms.

(C) *RESPECT FOR INDIVIDUAL DIFFERENCES*

People living with schizophrenia are unique individuals, each with their own specific needs, life circumstances, and biochemical sensitivities. Because of this, many mental health professionals now recognise that there need to be a range of different approaches to the way neuroleptic medications are used.

Research has shown that individual "tailoring" of medication is not only more effective therapeutically, but that it can also help to minimise problematic side-effects. Consequently, *every person should have their medications individually "tailored" to suit their particular needs and circumstances.* The following medication strategies may prove especially helpful to people who have had problems with "negative" symptoms related to their prescribed medication:

(i) *Once-A-Day Medication*

Though it is quite common for people to be instructed to take their neuroleptic medications in divided doses several times a day (e.g. with breakfast, lunch and dinner), many people might be better off taking *all* of their neuroleptic medication tablets at one time, shortly before going to bed at night.[133] There are no good medical reasons against doing this and it may have a number of advantages. In particular, taking neuroleptic medication at night may help to reduce tiredness or sleepiness during the day if these problems are related to the sedating side-effects of medication (it may also lessen the person's need for additional sleeping tablets at night).

(ii) *Low Dose Medication*

Research conducted over recent years has shown that people in acute psychotic episodes, as well as those on long-term "maintenance" treatment for schizophrenia, can often be treated effectively on doses of neuroleptic medication which are much lower than were once considered to be necessary.[134] In line with this realisation it appears that many people who have been on relatively high doses of medication for a long time may be able to manage just as well on much less.

With appropriate guidance and support, it is possible that some people can safely reduce their neuroleptic medication to as little as 20%-30% of the original dose. It is crucial to remember that **neuroleptic medication doses should always be reduced very slowly.** With the necessary support, reducing the dosage by 10% per week may be feasible for many people. (Some people who are on very low dose medication regimes may need to temporarily increase their routine dosage by taking extra medication temporarily if they are feeling particularly stressed.)

(iii) *Intermittent Medication*

Although most people take neuroleptic drugs on a continuous basis (i.e. tablets every day or regular injections), research has shown that some people may do well on an intermittent medication strategy. This approach involves a stable person gradually reducing and then ceasing all their neuroleptic drugs, and only commencing them again if and when they start to develop the "warning signs" which indicate that they may be at risk of becoming psychotic.[135] Some authorities estimate that at least 50% of all people being treated for schizophrenia could benefit from an intermittent medication strategy if they were appropriately supported.[136] Having good collaborative relationships with mental health professionals and other helpers is vital to the success of intermittent medication strategies.

(iv) *Use of "Minor Tranquillisers"*

Although they are not routinely used in the treatment of schizophrenia the so-called "minor tranquillisers", which include anti-anxiety benzodiazepine drugs such as alprazolam (Xanax), diazepam (Valium), and clonazepam (Rivotril), may be beneficial to some people, either on their own or in combination with neuroleptic medication.[136] These drugs can be particularly effective in helping to calm people who are agitated or hyper-aroused, the very feelings which may lead into self-protective withdrawal and "shut down". The "minor tranquilliser" drugs may also have an anti-psychotic effect for some people. Their major advantage is that they do not have any of the "negative" symptom side-effects of neuroleptic drugs.

Anyone considering using these drugs should be aware of the fact that most people will develop a tolerance to their beneficial effects (usually within a few months if they are taken continuously). Even more importantly, *dependence or addiction may develop.* Consequently, these drugs are probably only suitable for short-term "as needed" use, such as for acute anxiety or in the treatment of catatonic states.

(E) *REGULAR MONITORING*

It is important to remember that not only do medication

requirements differ from one person to another, but that *any given person's individual needs may change over time.* For example, a person's stress levels may begin to decrease as they develop greater confidence and self-esteem, which may in turn reduce their need for the "stress buffering" effects of neuroleptic medication. What this means in practice is that everyone taking these drugs should have their response to medication and their personal progress carefully monitored on a regular basis so that their drug regime can be modified and adjusted as required, in accordance with their ever-changing needs and circumstances.

A note about "new" neuroleptic drugs

In the past few years a number of new drugs have come into use which have been heralded as providing the first major breakthrough in the treatment of schizophrenia since neuroleptic drugs were introduced in the early 1950s. These medications, which include the so-called "atypical" neuroleptic Clozaril (clozapine) and the high-potency neuroleptic Risperdal (risperidone), are at present mainly used to treat people who have not responded favourably to various combinations and dosages of the more commonly prescribed drugs. Though it is probably too soon to draw any definite conclusions about their value, early evidence has suggested that they may produce fewer "negative" symptom side-effects than do the older drugs. In evaluating their possible usefulness a couple of things should be borne in mind, however. First of all, so far these drugs have mainly been given to people who have previously been on large (and sometimes *very* large) doses of medication, and possibly several different drugs. Consequently, if some improvement in a person's motivation and energy levels does occur on these drugs it is often difficult to tell if this is actually due to the effects of the new drug itself or if it is simply related to the fact that the person is no longer on such large doses of medication.

It should also be remembered that the so-called "placebo effect" may significantly influence the way people respond to *any* kind of treatment, and that this effect may be especially powerful when the treatment given is aimed at improving motivation, energy and morale. The following story very clearly illustrates just how great an influence a person's environment and the attitude of others can have in determining how they will respond to treatment – including drugs. The incident described occurred in the 1950s when tests were being conducted with chlorpromazine, the very first neuroleptic drug to be discovered. As part of these tests a long-term "chronic schizophrenic" patient named George had been chosen to ingest an experimental dose of Thorazine (chlorpromazine) every day:

> No one had paid George any attention for years. Now doctors, attendants and nurses all talked to him and watched eagerly to see what effect the drug would have. His condition improved rapidly. After only two weeks of the drug treatment he was moved to a ward for less disturbed patients where he took part in a number of activities. Soon he was doing so well that he was promoted again. By this time he had lively relationships with the other patients and many members of the hospital staff. He began to spend several hours a day with paints and clay, using them to express the rich fantasy life that had previously interested no one. His doctors marvelled. Attendants praised his skill. George was released from the hospital thirty-eight days after his first dose of Thorazine. While he was signing out he remembered that he had left something behind, went back to his room, and returned with an old sock. The puzzled attendant who asked to see it found thirty-eight Thorazine pills carefully stashed inside the sock.[137]

(Important Note: Any changes to medication regimes should always be made with the close supervision and support of appropriately qualified and experienced medical practitioners.)

(7) *Work for Recovery*

If there is one thing that the personal testimonies of countless numbers of people make clear, it is that courageous and persistent effort must be made by anyone who hopes to make progress in overcoming their problems. This is just as true in regard to mental health problems as it is to physical ones.

For various reasons many people find it difficult to accept that they must assume responsibility and work hard if their lives are to improve. In some cases their reluctance is due to the fact that they have never been expected or encouraged to be responsible for themselves before since others have always been prepared to take on that role. Furthermore, some people may have come to hope that eventually someone else – or something else – will come along and "fix" their problems for them. Sadly, many people have probably been encouraged to give up any idea that their own efforts could possibly make any real difference to their situation.

The turning point out of this kind of passive stance comes when people begin to discover that, no matter how "low" they are feeling, they *are* always able to do something – even if it is only very small to begin with – which will help them to bring about some small improvement in their life. As an example of this, Emma Pierce has described how she learnt that she could struggle to overcome her lethargy by pushing herself into doing small tasks, such as household chores:

> No matter how dopey, lethargic, depressed I felt, if I really wanted to, I could physically move my arms and legs and make them perform as I so ordered. This forced me to face the fact that the messy house was messy because, essentially, I didn't feel like cleaning it up . . . In time I was forced to recognise that when I commanded my limbs into action against lethargy, the lethargy left and after a period of time I felt better. Certainly a large part of feeling better, even happier, was the sense of achievement, both with what I had done, be it making a bed or sweeping a floor, and overcoming lethargy.[138]

One of the most common traps for people lies in deciding to wait until they feel better before they start doing things. Unfortunately, this attitude often means that nothing happens and nothing ever gets done! The simple fact is that many people discover that their mood and energy levels only begin to improve *after* they have started to become more active, rather than the other way around. For a while, at least, some people may literally need to *force* themselves into doing things – even when they don't feel like it – until they have started to break the grip that lethargy and inertia has had over them. One person gave this description of his personal fight against apathy:

> I couldn't stand inactivity, inertia, just sitting around
> not doing anything, so I would tend to very much force
> myself to read things, force myself to draw – no matter
> what – every day. I forced myself to do things which
> were hard even for other people. I found that doing
> this was what kept alive my self-respect. That battle was
> what really kept me together. I knew if I fought against
> apathy it would not overcome me, and to this very day
> I fight with all my might against it.

In the beginning, negative thoughts and self-doubt are among
the biggest and most difficult hurdles a person must overcome.
However, as Emma Pierce learnt from experience, it is absolutely
essential not to listen to or entertain such doubts. Instead a
person should make an effort to simply get on with doing things:

> Getting well will take time. But if you don't get started
> now, where will you be in six months from now? You
> cannot find your mental, physical and spiritual
> strength by sitting back and allowing other people to
> do things for you or to you. People doing things with
> you can be a great help, but you really must do the
> biggest part yourself. Get practical and get well. When
> you begin you will want to re-think your decisions a
> million times, looking for easier ways, looking for a
> quick cure-all. Don't! Once you have made a decision
> to do this or that to go forward, don't allow yourself to
> re-think the decision. You have examined all the pros
> and cons already. Re-examining is either looking for an
> excuse to let yourself out easily or an unnecessary
> chance that you will throw in the towel before you have
> even begun.[139]

Although mental health professionals and other helpers may
be able to provide invaluable encouragement, support and
guidance, the person who has "negative" symptoms must also do
as much as they are capable of if they are to achieve their optimal
level of functioning. *Because of the highly personal nature of these
problems, it may well turn out that the person's own efforts are the most
important ingredient of all to their recovery.*

(8) *Gradually Increase Activity and Responsibility*

Finding the energy and motivation to do things is often a problem. (It is worth remembering that this is true for *most* people at least some of the time!) For some people, there may be times when even the most basic daily activities are just too difficult – for example, during a period of post-psychotic "retreat", when "negative" symptoms are often at a very high level. It can be helpful to learn to expect this and to accept that during such times it is OK for a person to maintain only a very low level of activity temporarily. This can be compared to not expecting too much from someone who is recuperating from a serious physical illness or injury until they have started to get well and begun to regain some of their strength.

An important principle of recovery is for a person to begin doing things again a little at a time as soon as they are able and at whatever level they are capable of. It is important, however, for everyone to beware of just passively waiting for energy and motivation to return. Many people find that getting started is the hardest part; some people may actually need to force themselves into action. Once they have built up a level of energy and activity, however, many people find that it may be relatively easy to keep it going, at least for a while. Trying to do more than is realistic can be just as unwise as not trying to do anything at all, so it is best to begin doing things very gradually and then slowly increase the level of activity from there as confidence and ability grow.

The role of helpers is an important and often very difficult one. At certain times a person with severe "negative" symptoms may require a great deal of assistance from others. During such times, helpers may need to have only very modest expectations of what the person is capable of. They must beware of coming to *permanently* expect too little of the person, however, since this expectation itself can inhibit the return of their self-confidence and serve to reinforce dependency. For everyone concerned, a delicate "balancing act" is often involved: not expecting too much, on the one hand, but never settling for less than a person is realistically capable of, on the other.

(9) *Maintain a Structured Routine of Activity*

Without the imposed routine of employment some people tend to find themselves getting into the habit of just "drifting" from one day to the next without any clear direction or purpose. Though this may be acceptable for a time (such as during a period of much-needed rest and recuperation following a psychotic episode), it is unwise to allow it to continue for too long since it can eventually develop into a habit which becomes difficult to break.

Having specific things to do each day (e.g. household chores, voluntary work, social activities, study), or regular commitments (e.g. attending rehabilitation programs, counselling sessions) can all help to give each day a sense of focus, direction and purpose. Some people may find that doing things in a fairly similar way each day at set times provides them with a reassuring sense of order and predictability (things shouldn't be so predictable that they become boring, however!). Professor Agnes Hatfield has explained why routine and order can be of particular benefit to people living with schizophrenia:

> Structure and predictability in the external world help compensate for the unpredictability of the inner world. Daily routines give pattern and a sense of order to life. By knowing what to expect, the person with schizophrenia can prepare himself and thus exert a degree of control over events. Stress and anxiety lessen when events lose their sense of arbitrariness and an appearance of consistency emerges.[140]

Organising and following a simple routine of daily activities helps to counteract the temptation to drift aimlessly through the day. For example, getting up at the same (reasonable) time each morning and doing some simple physical exercise (such as a twenty minute walk, basic callisthenics, yoga, etc.) gets the day off to a good start. After a while, as new habits are developed, it will usually become easier to wake up and get going. Paying close attention to small things, and trying to remain focused on the "here and now", can also help to reduce feelings of aimlessness, as John Beavis discovered:

> A good way to deal with the oceans of time on which one feels adrift is to focus very clearly on no more than the next five minutes, to live in the present to an exaggerated degree. This way of living presents

> hundreds of short, insignificant tasks, but if these are attended to the feeling of being adrift will disappear as the finer details of life – meals, money, comb, clean socks, stamps, etc. – find their place and help to ease the transition from experience to experience. Time is then so much less frustrating and one is able to quietly "swim" across the ocean instead of merely drifting.[141]

Some people allow themselves to fall into bad habits such as sleeping excessively, spending many hours watching TV, or just daydreaming. Though these activities may serve a useful purpose at times (they can provide a temporary escape from excessive stimulation and emotional intensity, for example) there comes a point when they no longer have any constructive value and serve only to foster a trance-like state of mindlessness and avoidance.

Though breaking such habits can be very difficult – especially if they have started to become addictions – doing so can help to increase the amount of energy a person has for living. Anyone who has attempted to encourage somebody to "kick" such habits knows that their efforts may elicit angry indignation or hostility from the person whose routines are being challenged. Such a reaction coming from someone with "negative" symptoms such as apathy or "blunted affect" is noteworthy, however, since it indicates that the person's capacity to feel and express strong emotions is not entirely lost. (Since anger is a form of emotional energy, it is worth asking where this energy goes when a person is left to "blob out" in front of the TV.)

(10) *Find A Balanced Level of Stimulation*

Excessive social stimulation and pressure to perform is stressful and often leads to withdrawal as a coping strategy. Some people may withdraw too much, however, and then find themselves suffering from the effects of under-stimulation, which itself can contribute to an increase in "negative" symptoms. Everybody must try to find a comfortable balance between over-stimulation and under-stimulation according to their own personal needs and degree of sensitivity. *The "ideal" balance between too much stimulation and too little is very individual.* Thus, a relatively high level of stimulation suits some people, whilst others are probably likely to do better with a great deal less.

The ideal balance of stimulation may also change over time as a person's inner and outer circumstances change. For example, during the recuperative phase which follows a psychotic episode (post-psychotic "retreat") many people are hypersensitive and need to be protected from excessive social and emotional stimulation. Later on, as they slowly emerge from this phase, a gradually increasing level of activity and responsibility may be needed to provide the social and emotional stimulation which help to promote recovery.

Professor Manfred Bleuler believes that people with a diagnosis of schizophrenia usually do best with an optimal balance between stimulating activity which allows for the natural unfolding of their abilities, and a degree of routine and order, which helps them to achieve and maintain a state of calmness and control.[142]

(11) *Cultivate Patience and Persistence*

Recovering from "negative" symptoms is often a slow and gradual process. Sometimes it is so painfully slow that it may seem as if nothing at all is happening. It is worth keeping in mind that just because nothing *seems* to be happening does not necessarily mean that nothing *is* happening. Subtle processes of mental and emotional healing which are invisible may be occurring "below the surface", and it can take some time before any significant change starts to become obvious.

Patience, persistence and the willingness to "hang in" are absolutely vital ingredients in anyone's struggle with "negative" symptoms. The lives of many courageous people have shown again and again that human beings do have an innate ability to pick themselves up and start all over even after they have experienced what feels like total defeat. Keeping the following points in mind can help to foster patience during what may be a long and difficult struggle:

- Learn to recognise, value and reward the smallest signs of progress, even if they seem almost insignificant. Each and every small step, however slow, fans the precious flames of hope.
- Redefine "success". Instead of setting impossible goals, adopt the attitude that doing things a little at a time at the best level presently possible is itself a real achievement.

- Remember that people recover very slowly and gradually from any type of injury, and that "invisible" wounds, too, take time to heal.
- Acknowledge the willingness to make an attempt at doing things, even if these efforts seem rather slow or clumsy at times.
- Remember the old Chinese saying: "A journey of one thousand miles begins with a single step".

It is important for helpers to always remember that people's perception of time and the progress of change can be very relative. The following anecdote, related by the psychotherapist Frieda Fromm-Reichman, clearly illustrates such relativity:

> [A patient's] progress seemed so exceedingly slow to me that at times I asked myself whether there was any progress at all or whether I was handling him incorrectly and should transfer him to a colleague who might be able to be useful to the patient in a shorter time. One day this patient commented spontaneously: "Things are going surprisingly well between us except that they are going too fast. If only you wouldn't rush me so that I would not have to go so rapidly."[143]

(12) *Practise Gentleness*

When energy and motivation remain at a low level for a while it is easy for a person to start becoming self-critical, especially if this type of problem is new. People who have previously had energy and motivation often tend to "give themselves a hard time" if they are not being as active as they feel they should be. Though it is quite understandable this kind of self-criticism can be very destructive, especially as it may contribute to increasing despair and demoralisation, and then into the "vicious circle" of "negative" symptoms.

Learning to be gentle with oneself can help recovery greatly. Temporarily lowering all expectations and setting modest, achievable goals may be difficult for some people at first, but it is often vital, especially early on when motivation and energy levels are at their lowest and the tendency to self-criticism is highest. Acknowledging and valuing small achievements, and accepting that gradual, step-by-step progress is good, are essential attitudes.

A helpful motto to adopt is that "two steps forward and one step backwards is OK".

(13) *Adopt A Healthy Lifestyle*

Some people troubled by "negative" symptoms allow themselves to fall into self-destructive habits of living such as eating poorly, sleeping erratically, over-indulging in cigarettes, coffee and alcohol, or even abusing prescribed medications. Some people may even resort to using stimulant drugs such as caffeine (in tea and coffee) or amphetamines ("speed") in an attempt to counteract their apathy and lack of energy.

In the long run these habits are only likely to make matters worse. On the other hand, anything which helps to increase a person's level of fitness and health is bound to be helpful. Thus, a well-balanced diet, some regular exercise, adequate rest, healthy recreation, and positive thinking can all contribute to the development of a sense of well-being and stamina which will be helpful to anyone struggling with "negative" symptoms. The following points are especially relevant:

- Vitamin and mineral deficiencies and untreated physical health problems can contribute to a person's lack of energy and low motivation. It is a good idea to have a thorough examination by a competent medical practitioner at least once a year in order to detect and receive treatment for any possible problems in these areas.

- Some people living with schizophrenia seem to need more rest and sleep than the average person requires. Getting adequate rest and sleep is therefore very important. On the other hand, however, sleeping *more* than is really necessary tends to have the effect of draining a person's energy and inducing lethargy and mental dullness.

- Exercise gives people energy. Even a small amount of regular exercise is better than none. For people who are out of the habit of exercising, or who have very little energy, a short (20-30 minute) walk every day is a good way to begin.

- Smoking cigarettes is now known to have many adverse effects on physical health. Apart from this, nicotine may also cause a decrease in the concentration of neuroleptic medication in a smoker's bloodstream. Some researchers believe that *some people may smoke cigarettes in order to help reduce problems with medication side-effects such as sedation or lethargy.*[144] People on neuroleptic drugs who stop or cut down on cigarette smoking sometimes experience an *increase* in "negative" symptoms related to medication side-effects. (Any concerns about these issues should be discussed with the person who is responsible for prescribing the neuroleptic drugs. Note that it is possible for a person who wants to quit smoking to continue getting nicotine by using nicotine-enriched chewing gum or skin patches.)

(14) *Utilise Counselling or Psychotherapy*

Although some mental health professionals continue to question the value of psychotherapy for people with a diagnosis of schizophrenia, recent research reported in the *American Journal of Psychiatry* has shown that psychotherapy provided by skilful and empathic therapists can be specifically helpful in reducing such "negative" symptoms as apathy and withdrawal.[145]

Counselling or psychotherapy can be very helpful to people with "negative" symptoms by providing a safe, supportive relationship in which frustrations and concerns can be shared and understood. Counselling can help with common problems such as low self-esteem, loss of self-confidence, feelings of demoralisation, unresolved grieving over lost opportunities, and the effects of stigma. Post-Traumatic Stress Disorder (PTSD) and the kind of depression which sometimes occur in association with "negative" symptoms (see Part One), may be especially responsive to skilfully conducted counselling. (It is important to remember that the neuroleptic medications used in the treatment of schizophrenia cannot directly help with any of these problems, all of which might be contributing significantly to a person's "negative" symptoms.)

For people whose extreme sensitivity makes them wary of allowing themselves to get too close to others, a trusting relationship with a therapist can provide a safe opportunity to work on issues of trust and intimacy. One woman explained how important her relationship with her therapist had been in helping her to break through her fear of people so that she could become more confident of her place in the human world:

> When I become close to someone ... I become
> frightened and run frantically from the very thing I
> desire most – to be close to another human being. All
> my life I held this desire hidden so far inside me that
> even I could not see it. I think I have always known it
> was there, but I was afraid to consider the possibility for
> fear of rejection or scorn. ... I often felt at odds with
> my therapist until I could see that he was a real person
> and he related to me and I to him, not only as patient
> and therapist, but as human beings. Eventually I began
> to discover I was a real person, not just an outsider
> looking in on the world. ... I had drawn so far inside
> myself and so far away from the world, I had to be
> shown not only that the world was safe but also that I
> belonged to it, that I was in fact a person. ... But none
> of that can happen without the all-important but ever
> elusive element of trust.[146]

A trusting relationship with a therapist or counsellor can
provide an ideal opportunity for a person to work on issues to do
with the way they handle their feelings. Some people may need
the guidance of a skilled counsellor in order to actually get "in
touch" again with long-suppressed feelings. In some cases, it
seems, people who develop "negative" symptoms may have gotten
into the habit of "bottling up" painful feelings and attempting to
hide them away.[147] One of the most valuable things that a
counsellor can do in such cases is to help a person to accept that
all of their feelings are OK – even painful or "scary" ones such as
fear and anger – and to teach them how to express these feelings
in a safe and constructive way.

Good counselling also provides on-going support and
encouragement which helps a person to develop realistically
hopeful expectations and plans for their future. Having someone
who constantly and actively relates to their "healthy" aspects, and
who continually emphasises their strengths and abilities, inevitably
encourages anyone who is sincerely trying to grow and develop.

(15) *Learn Effective Coping Skills*
In time, many people with a diagnosis of schizophrenia can use
their experience and a process of trial-and-error to learn a range

of coping skills and strategies which can be helpful in reducing, controlling – and possibly even preventing – "positive" psychotic symptoms such as delusions and hallucinations.[148] Acquiring such coping skills may also help to reduce or even prevent some "negative" symptoms by making it less necessary for a person to use *excessive* social withdrawal and "emotional shut-down" as their sole means of self-protection. In addition, anyone who has learnt effective coping skills is likely to feel more self-confident and therefore be less inclined to "hide themselves away" in order to avoid stressful situations. Among the wide range of practical coping skills which many people may be able to learn, the following may be especially valuable:

(a) *Stress management*
These are basic "survival skills" which every person living with schizophrenia should learn. They include:

- Learning to identify specific causes of stress. These are sometimes highly individual (e.g. involving things that most people may not find particularly stressful).
- Learning to recognise the subtle "warning signals" (also called prodromal symptoms) which a person may experience if exposed to more stress than they can easily handle.
- Learning stress management techniques. These may include: relaxation techniques, positive "self talk", building up self-esteem, maintaining a healthy lifestyle, and selectively avoiding stressful situations.

(b) *Techniques for controlling or preventing "positive" symptoms*
Research has shown that in time many people do eventually learn how to prevent or reduce the intensity of their hallucinatory "voices"[149] and delusional thoughts.[150] Some of the most commonly used techniques include:

- Distraction: deliberately shifting attention away from "voices" or troubling thoughts and on to something else (e.g. watching TV, listening to music, doing chores, hobbies, sleeping, going out).
- Social contact: spending time with other people (with or without speaking).
- Physical activity: walking, jogging, playing sports, exercise.

- Relaxation: listening to soothing music, progressive relaxation techniques, guided imagery, meditation, walking in nature.
- Mental control: learning to deliberately suppress unpleasant or distressing thoughts, consciously focusing attention on positive thoughts or pleasant memories, telling negative "voices" to stop or go away, or simply refusing to listen to them.

The following anecdote illustrates how one man taught himself to prevent his delusional thoughts from beginning by using selective avoidance (of certain people or topics) whenever he recognised that he was beginning to feel "worked up" (a personal "warning signal"):

> It is a matter of learning from experience. In my case, I have realised that certain situations tend to bring on symptoms. Of course, there is a sensitivity in myself and I have to try to harden my emotions and cut myself off from potentially dangerous situations. For example, I now tend to avoid contact with people who antagonise me or whom I seem to upset. I sometimes find myself getting worked up about some topic – it might be something political or religious, for example ... At times like these, when I get worked up, I often experience a slight recurrence of delusional thoughts. I begin to notice coincidences which otherwise I would not have noticed. I might meet someone I hadn't expected to see. Then I might start testing some delusional theory. Let me see whether that car turns the corner behind me. If so, is it still there several turnings later? Then it must be following me! I now feel that I have sufficient knowledge of myself to know that this kind of thinking is dangerous. I can control my mind sufficiently to prevent such thoughts getting out of control and destroying my inner self.[151]

A person's need for sustained high levels of neuroleptic medication, with the attendant risk of troublesome side-effects, can sometimes be significantly reduced if they are able to learn effective non-drug coping strategies for preventing or controlling psychotic symptoms.[152]

(16) *Cultivate Self-Esteem*

People living with schizophrenia have often had their ability to believe in themselves very badly damaged – if not completely shattered – by what they have been through, and by the many negative messages they have received about their worth as a person as a result of the stigma attached to being diagnosed with a mental illness. Fear and demoralisation may eventually force such people into a self-conscious avoidance of involvement with others – and perhaps with life generally – and may contribute significantly to the persistence of "negative" symptoms.

Good self-esteem provides the "solid ground" upon which a new life can be built. It is also a vital source of the inner strength which is needed by anyone who must fight the many battles that will inevitably be faced now and in the future. Consequently, *rebuilding self-esteem and self-confidence is crucial to recovery*. Regaining confidence and a sense of self-worth takes time and a great deal of effort but it can be done, as many people have proven. The following are some of the important factors which can help a person in this challenging task:

(a) *Acknowledge that there is a problem*

Many people feel ashamed and guilty about having poor self-esteem and low self-confidence. If they are intense, such feelings may even prevent a person from facing and dealing with these issues. Though it can be difficult, finding the courage to honestly admit to having these problems is essential to beginning the process of change.

(b) *Guard against internalising social stigma*

The self-esteem of people living with schizophrenia is often badly affected by the many negative attitudes that exist about "mental illness" in the general community. All people who have received a psychiatric diagnosis need to be constantly on guard against the danger of internalising this stigma and developing negative attitudes and beliefs about themselves as a result.

(c) *Find an identity other than "mental patient"*

Over time some people may gradually come to identify themselves more and more fully with the diagnosis they have been given until, at last, they begin to see themselves as being totally identified with this "label". In order to avoid ever becoming "a full-time mental patient", it is important that a person strives to base their sense of identity and personal value on their *whole* self, always remembering that schizophrenia is only *one part* of their life.

(d) *Affirm positive qualities and achievements*

One of the most effective ways to repair damaged self-esteem is for a person to constantly work at recognising and affirming all of their positive achievements and qualities – no matter how small or insignificant they may appear to be. In doing this it is especially important to acknowledge and affirm even the most subtle, but nevertheless important, personal qualities such as gentleness, honesty, sensitivity, kindness and humility – the very qualities which make every person unique. In a society which places so much emphasis on *material* success and achievement, anybody can experience fragile self-esteem. It can be comforting to remember that ultimately a human being's worth is determined not by what they do or what they own, but by what kind of person they are!

(e) *Remember that everyone experiences failure*

People who have low self-esteem sometimes become so afraid of failure that they will do almost anything to avoid it. This may mean that they avoid doing practically anything which might involve even the slightest risk of them being unsuccessful. A person's irrational belief that failing at anything only confirms how truly worthless they are can eventually become a trap which totally paralyses creative action. In order to break this cycle it is essential to understand that nobody is perfect and that every human being inevitably experiences failure from time to time. Kathleen Gallo has described the very liberating effect this realisation had on her:

> After all the struggling I have done ... I am now accepting enough of myself, and know and like myself well enough, to be able to encounter failure without it having the catastrophic effect it once inevitably had on me. I now understand that failure does not mean that I am worthless. Rather, it is an indication that I too am a human being and, as such, I will occasionally experience failure along with many successes on the road of my life.[153]

(f) *Utilise counselling or psychotherapy*
Many counsellors and therapists are able to help people build up their confidence and self-esteem using a range of techniques specifically designed for dealing with these problems. Developing a trusting relationship with a counsellor can help a person to feel safe enough to "open up" and speak frankly about the various things that are troubling them. Many people who have begun to regain self-confidence and self-esteem speak of the importance of having a therapist who was able to believe in them when they were unable to believe in themselves.

(g) *Practise positive "self talk"*
Everyone talks to themselves in their own mind about what they are feeling, experiencing and doing. Such "self talk" has a powerful effect on a person's mood, self-esteem and self-confidence. People with low self-esteem often engage in negative "self talk" with which they constantly "put themselves down" by telling themselves they are bad, worthless, inferior, a failure, and so on. With practice, most people can eventually learn to reduce this negative "self talk" and replace it with positive "self talk". Because positive "self talk" affirms and reinforces a person's positive qualities and abilities, in time it inevitably helps to build up self-esteem and enhance self-confidence.

(h) *Practise dignity and self-respect*
People who don't feel good about themselves sometimes tend to become increasingly careless about their appearance, grooming, personal hygiene and social behaviour. Some people eventually "let themselves go" and abandon any attempt to maintain their dignity and self-respect. This can develop into a vicious circle because a person's behaviour inevitably has an effect on the way they feel. Changing these habits can be very difficult, especially if there doesn't seem to be any point to it. However, experience shows that if a person does make a sincere effort to take better care of themselves they will eventually begin to feel more positive. In time these efforts may even lead them to a whole new appreciation of their inherent dignity and worth as a unique human being.

(17) *Find a Meaning and Purpose in Life*
One of the greatest challenges that must be faced by many people whose life has been deeply affected by schizophrenia lies in

coming to terms with the fact that the hopes and plans that once guided life and gave it meaning, purpose and direction may no longer be feasible. Unless these losses can be compensated for, life may begin to lack real meaning and purpose. If this continues for too long, an aimless drifting can begin which may eventually turn into a downward spiral toward despair and demoralisation. Consequently, *regaining a sense of meaning and purpose in life is absolutely essential to overcoming many "negative" symptoms.*

Though finding the energy and motivation to break out of a state of alienation and despair is difficult it is possible, with effort, for a person to change such a situation. In the beginning, even very small and apparently trivial things can play an important role in helping to restore the sense of purpose which has been lost from a person's life. As an example, some researchers found that when the residents of an old people's home were given some potted plants to look after, their death rate decreased. Something as simple as caring for a few plants gave these people's lives a renewed sense of purpose which had a beneficial effect on their health! Doing things for others can be especially effective in enhancing a person's sense of usefulness and purpose. Dr Bernie Siegel has described what happened when a counsellor encouraged her cancer patients to start doing voluntary work:

> Whenever she could make no progress with her clients, she would send them downstairs to enlist as volunteers – and guess what? [They] got better fast! Even borderline individuals improved markedly. Their grasp on reality, self-esteem and purpose for living improved as they gave of themselves in unselfish ways that felt good to them. Volunteers live longer and have fewer illnesses.[154]

Finding sufficient motivation and energy to begin doing things is often very difficult at first. And yet – perhaps somewhere deep down inside themselves – most people probably always hold on to at least a few small and flickering "sparks" of interest which might yet be rekindled. Like an oasis in a barren desert these "sparks" may be a precious resource which preserves and, in time, helps to bring forth new life. Even if a person can only remain interested in something for very short periods initially, protecting and nurturing this interest is important; it might eventually provide a vital "lifeline" to recovery.

Even very brief periods spent appreciating and enjoying the beauty of nature, music, art, poetry, hobbies, cooking, eating, simple human companionship – virtually anything that "turns a person on" (however slightly) may help to revive and restore their depleted spirit. It does not really matter if the things that appear to stimulate and interest someone are "unusual" or "unrealistic" pursuits. As long as it is healthy and constructive, any interest that kindles at least a little enthusiasm is worth encouraging.

Some people may find that following their *real* interests leads them down a very different path to the one they had mapped out in earlier life. In some instances, having the courage to follow such a new direction to wherever it may lead might just mean the difference between a life of satisfaction and growth and one of stagnation.

(18) *Confront New Situations and Responsibilities*

Whilst sensible precautions are a vital aspect of self-care, some people may succumb to the temptation of trying to keep themselves "wrapped in cotton wool" in order to avoid experiencing pain and fear. This can happen, for example, when a person continually resists allowing any change to occur in their life simply because they fear it will lead to anxiety and discomfort. Anyone who attempts to live this way for too long is bound to retard their emotional growth and development. Sensible risk-taking is important in *every* person's life, as the sayings "nothing ventured, nothing gained" and "no pain, no gain" reflect.

Anyone who has finally achieved a degree of stability in their life may be understandably reluctant to risk "upsetting the apple cart" by making too many changes. However, there are times in everyone's life when being prepared to take a step into the unknown may be the only way to move forward. From time to time it is good for people living with schizophrenia to be faced with new situations and new responsibilities, and perhaps even with some unexpected changes in their environment and routines.[155] For example: meeting with new people or going to new places; finding the courage to discuss personal matters with a friend or counsellor; applying for a job or a course of study; expressing feelings that have long been "bottled up"; changing to a lower dose or a different type of medication (with appropriate guidance and support). Such changes can all help to "shake a person up", and may even reveal the existence of hidden resources and strengths which are not being used.

Naturally, very sensitive timing is essential to the success of these strategies. A person must be ready for these kinds of challenges if they are to really benefit from them. When they are ready, however, such changes may be very beneficial to a person who has become "stuck" in an unhealthy stability. Sometimes they may even reveal an unexpected way out of a "comfortable rut" of fixed habits and rigid behaviour patterns.

(19) *Beware of Depression*

For the many reasons described in Part One, depression ranging in severity from fairly mild to quite severe is a common problem among people living with schizophrenia.[156] Some of the main symptoms of depression, such as loss of interest and pleasure and lack of energy, closely resemble "negative" symptoms. Consequently, depression can quite easily be overlooked if the person's depressive-type symptoms are automatically considered to be symptoms of schizophrenia.

Skilled professional assessment is needed in order to reliably diagnose depression in a person who also has "negative" symptoms. If depression is diagnosed a number of different forms of treatment may be effective, depending on the type, severity and suspected cause (or causes) of the depression. If any of a person's "negative" type symptoms are actually symptoms of depression they should disappear in time as the depression is successfully treated. In most cases, one or more of the following approaches are likely to be helpful:

(a) *Medication Adjustment*

"Akinetic" depression is a type of depression caused by neuroleptic medication.[157] A person can develop "akinetic" depression even though they may have no noticeable parkinsonian side-effect symptoms such as tremor, shuffling gait and mask-like face. Anyone experiencing "akinetic" depression is likely to look or feel at least a bit drowsy, however. *The presence of this type of depression should be ruled out before any other possible causes of depression are considered.* The simple reason for this is that "psychological" forms of treatment for depression are not likely to be very effective if the *real* cause of the problem is the person's neuroleptic medication. If a person is diagnosed as having "akinetic" depression, the following strategies have been recommended:

● Reducing the total dosage of neuroleptic medication;
● Taking antiparkinsonian "side-effect" medications such as Cogentin (benztropine), Kemadrin (procyclidine), or Artane (benzhexol).

It has been suggested by some authorities that these measures should be considered for any person with a diagnosis of schizophrenia who becomes depressed.[158] Sometimes, the only reliable way to tell if the depression is caused by neuroleptic drugs is to note the effect on the person of a trial on antiparkinsonian medication:

> If a schizophrenic patient becomes depressed during a course of anti-psychotic drug therapy, the clinician should first consider the possibility that this is a "toxic" drug effect. The fact that the depression may be "understandable" or that the [patient] himself attributes it to circumstances should not be accepted at face value. The response to a brief course of antiparkinsonian drug should distinguish between akinetic depression and depression due to some other cause.[159]

If the depression is caused by medication the person's mood should improve *rapidly* as a result of the strategies mentioned above. *Some people may improve dramatically following the administration of a single test dose of antiparkinsonian medication.* If this happens, it virtually proves that the depression was indeed medication-induced.

If the minimal effective dose of neuroleptic medication is always used, problems with drug-induced "akinetic" depression and other medication side-effects are likely to be minimised.

(b) *Psychosocial Treatment*

As outlined in Part One, many of the possible causes of depression are *psychological* in nature. Stigma, shame and guilt, damaged self-esteem, loss of hope for the future, and demoralisation can all push a person into a state of depression. In such cases, identifying the various factors which are causing the depression is the first priority. Following this, every effort should be made to eliminate them, as far as it is possible to do so. For example, continuing high levels of pressure on a person to perform and achieve (whether this pressure comes from the depressed person themselves or from others) should be reduced to a more realistic level; stigma can be reduced by providing positive education about schizophrenia which aims to dispel the "doom and gloom" so often associated with this diagnosis; shame and guilt may be alleviated by open sharing with others who have had similar experiences.

Counselling or supportive psychotherapy can be very helpful. The empathic support and understanding provided by a sensitive counsellor helps to reduce a person's feelings of isolation and aloneness. At the same time, counselling can assist a person to develop realistic hope as well as providing on-going support for their personal efforts aimed at improving life generally. Certain types of therapy (e.g. cognitive behaviour therapy) aim specifically at helping people to reduce their habitual patterns of negative "self talk" and to replace it with positive "self talk". Doing this has been shown to be a highly effective form of treatment for many types of depression.

(c) *Antidepressant medication*
Some people may experience depression which is severe enough for them to require treatment with antidepressant medication. In such cases, special care should be taken because antidepressant drugs may sometimes interfere with the therapeutic activity of neuroleptic medication.[160] Regular and careful monitoring of the person's mental state will help to minimise the risk of any undesirable complications.

(20) *Guard Against the "Seduction of Madness"*
Many people who have experienced psychosis know that, in addition to the distressing and frightening aspects of this experience, there may have been others which were not so unpleasant. Though confusion and fear may have eventually come to predominate, people can often remember moments or experiences during a psychotic episode which felt exciting, exhilarating, liberating or creative. Some psychotic symptoms may have even had enjoyable or rewarding aspects, at least for a

while. "Grandiose delusions", for example, may have made a person feel very important, special or powerful, and some "auditory hallucinations" ("voices") may have been experienced as loving companions or trustworthy guides.[161]

The fact that some psychotic experiences may be comforting or enjoyable raises the possibility that they might sometimes tend to "seduce" a person away from the world of everyday reality and into the "other world" of psychosis. This power of this "seduction" is likely to be especially great if everyday reality is slow, painful and boring – which it often is for people living with schizophrenia, especially during the long and often agonisingly slow process of recuperation and recovery.[162]

As well as providing an escape from excruciating boredom some psychotic symptoms may offer the tempting promise of an "instant" – though illusory – solution to difficult personal problems. A person who feels very lonely, for example, may understandably be tempted by the familiar and ever-present companionship provided by friendly "voices"; people with low self-esteem may longingly remember the feeling of importance and confidence that accompanied their "grandiose delusions". In an attempt to regain such "desirable" psychotic symptoms some people may refuse to take their prescribed neuroleptic medication. Others may even begin using social or illicit drugs in an effort to rekindle psychotic experiences which they find enjoyable.

Some people who appear apathetic and unmotivated may have become so absorbed in their private "inner" reality that they have virtually severed contact with the outer world. Indeed, anyone who allows themselves to become preoccupied with voices, visions or delusional beliefs will inevitably have difficulty participating fully in the ordinary world with other people. Consequently, everyone who is facing a struggle with "negative" symptoms must be constantly on guard against the seductive "gravitational pull" of psychotic reality.

The best protection against the "seduction of madness" comes from having a life which provides sufficient enjoyment, interest, satisfaction and stimulation. Although this may seem like a very tall order – and it is in the beginning – everything that strengthens and enriches a person's "everyday" reality will inevitably help to make the "psychotic" reality less attractive. Building up self-confidence and self-esteem, for example, will increase a person's ability to develop satisfying relationships with ordinary people instead of with "voices". In time and with persistent effort, the growing realisation that life in *this* world is possible and that it can be enjoyable will inevitably reduce the power of the "other world" to seduce and to hold.

(21) *Respect and Nurture Spirituality*

In traditional cultures it is commonly accepted that mental health is founded upon spirituality. In earlier times Western societies, too, understood that a person's spiritual life plays a vital role in determining their state of mental health and well-being. In fact the ancient Greek word "psyche", from which we derive such modern terms as "psychology" and "psychotherapy", was originally understood to refer to the human soul or spirit. Although it is seldom realised today, the word "psychiatry" itself literally means "the healing of the soul".

Researchers who have studied the deepest inner aspects of psychotic experience have often concluded that during their psychotic episodes many people undergo very profound and intensely spiritual crises.[163] Failure to recognise and properly resolve such crises can contribute to long-standing and disabling personal conflict. In writing about her own experiences Patricia Deegan has described the "faltering of the spirit" which often lies at the heart of the state of demoralisation so common among people with "negative" symptoms. She compared it to the "dark night of the soul" experience spoken of by some Christian mystics:

> All of us who have experienced catastrophic illness and disability know this experience of anguish and despair. It is living in darkness without hope, without a past or a future. ... Anguish is a death from which there appears to be no resurrection. It is inertia which paralyses the will to do and to accomplish because there is no hope. It is being truly disabled, not by a disease or injury, but by despair. This part of the recovery process is a dark night in which even God was felt to have abandoned us. For some of us this dark night lasts moments, days, or months. For others it lasts for years. For others, the despair and anguish may never end.[164]

In such circumstances the "spirit" that normally animates a person and gives them life may seem to have all but disappeared. In many traditional cultures this state would possibly be diagnosed as a symptom of "soul loss", and various shamanic rituals and spiritual techniques might be employed in an attempt to "retrieve" the person's lost soul.[165] Although such ideas are completely foreign to most Westerners, it is possible that people whose "negative" symptoms are caused or exacerbated by demoralisation, loss of meaning and direction, and low self-worth may benefit significantly from spiritual beliefs and practices that address these specific problems. *To the extent that true spirituality can help to restore a person's sense of personal worth and foster within them a belief that their life has some meaning and purpose, it can be a very positive and powerful healing influence.*

Some people who receive a diagnosis of schizophrenia have probably always had a deeply sensitive concern with religious and spiritual questions. Many others find that experiencing psychosis has forced them to confront the deepest and most basic questions of human life, such as: "Who am I really?", "What should I do with my life?" and – especially – "Why has this happened to me?" Because no simple solutions are available to such questions, the answers must inevitably be sought at the deepest levels. As a consequence of an intensive personal struggle to find answers to questions such as these some people may even experience an awakening of their long-neglected or dormant spirituality.

Whether or not a person chooses to accept a specific religious belief system and its observances – such as attending a particular church or temple – they may still benefit in a very real and tangible way from the cultivation of their spirituality. At its most basic level spirituality involves developing a *living* relationship or connection with God (some people may prefer to use terms such as a "Higher Power", "Higher Self" or the "Source of Life"). Most importantly, it also involves adopting a set of values which are based on something beyond mere materialistic concerns, self-gratification and self-centredness.

Considerable research and the testimonies of numerous people have shown that a person's spiritual beliefs and practices may be a significant source of comfort, strength and guidance. Spirituality can help recovery in many ways, such as by helping a person to cope with stress more effectively, providing a source of forgiveness, enhancing self-esteem, and fostering a sense of acceptance and belonging. In a recent study of people who were doing well in recovery from severe mental illness 48% said that their spiritual beliefs or practices were central to their success.[166] Most importantly, the feeling of utter personal inadequacy and worthlessness which so often has a crippling effect on people living with schizophrenia may be overcome as a person develops a sense of their ultimate spiritual worth. For those who have struggled with the pain and stigma of "mental illness" the key to recovering a sense of personal value, Patricia Deegan believes, lies in discovering the precious "spark of the divine" which lives eternally within every human being:

> You may have been diagnosed with a mental illness, but you are not an illness. You are a human being whose life is precious and is of infinite value. . . . You are precious and good. You are not trash to be discarded or a broken object that must be fixed. You are not insane. You do not belong in institutions for the rest of your life. You don't belong on the streets. . . . You are a human being. You carry within you a precious flame, a spark of the divine. . . . You were born to love and to be loved. That's your birthright. Mental illness cannot take that from you. Nobody can take that from you.[167]

Part Three

The Dark Side
of the Moon

ADJUSTING TO CHANGE, LETTING GO, ACCEPTING

Everybody who experiences and struggles with schizophrenia and "negative" symptoms has a long, hard road to travel. In the beginning the journey forward may seem too difficult, perhaps even impossible. When any hoped for improvements do eventually occur, they may be painfully slow in coming. And yet, with time and courageous persistent effort, many people *do* eventually begin to emerge from the darkness into a new and more hopeful way of living and being.

The experience of beginning to "thaw out" after a long period of feeling numb and cut off from life can itself be painful and difficult. As they begin to emerge, some people may find it hard to see how far they've come and only be aware of how much further they have still to go. And, as a person regains energy and clarity, they will inevitably be faced with many more questions, choices and responsibilities than they have been used to dealing with. This in itself can be frightening and bewildering, especially for those who are still very fragile and lacking in confidence. As they think about the struggle that still lies ahead of them, the question "Is it worth it?" may arise again and again.

Like many others, Patricia Ruocchio found this "in between" existence so difficult that at times she wished she had been able to remain in her previous unchanging state:

> Perhaps the hardest part of beginning to recover . . . is passing back and forth from one part to the other – the movement from sanity into insanity. I find this most difficult because it is excruciating to be grounded and then to feel this pulled out from under you suddenly or gradually crumbled under stress. Often I wish that they had left me in the world of insanity where everything is predictable, all is the same, and nothing changes.[168]

Recovering from severe "negative" symptoms may feel like a mixed blessing to many people whilst they are still adjusting to new levels of energy, changing roles and expectations, and increased responsibility. For the person undergoing these changes, as well as for helpers and carers, many difficult challenges must be faced and many demanding adjustments made. Without doubt, this is a time when *everybody* involved needs much gentleness, patience, tolerance and support.

Adjusting to Change

The gradual "unblocking" of a person's energy and emotions, combined with their growing confidence in expressing themselves, sometimes leads to situations which are difficult to deal with in a constructive way.[169] This is especially likely if a significant increase in a person's level of energy and motivation has occurred relatively quickly (for example, as a result of adjustments to neuroleptic medication regimes so that "negative" symptom side-effects are minimised).

One situation which is often very difficult to handle may occur as a person begins to feel and express strong emotions, such as anger. Recovering people sometimes direct such feelings at themselves, at family members or mental health professionals, or even at life in general which has seemed so unfair. Patricia Deegan has explained one of the many possible reasons for anger:

> You feel angry because you have been diagnosed with a major mental illness. You feel angry because all your friends are doing normal stuff like going to school, going on dates, and dreaming their dreams. You feel, "Why me? Why has this happened to me?"[170]

Although expressions of anger can be frightening and difficult to deal with, some therapists believe that *controlled* anger may actually be helpful to the recovery process.[171] As long as a person can avoid the trap of becoming "stuck" in their anger, its vital energy may help to provide them with the impetus and momentum needed in their struggle to continue moving forward. Angry indignation may even be crucial to a person's efforts to protect and preserve their dignity and sense of self-control which are under threat from the many negative and stigmatising messages that every person living with schizophrenia inevitably encounters. Such understandable anger might even be compared to that which drives reformers to fight social injustice.

As a person begins to feel and express their emotions more and more, both they and others face the challenge of learning to cope with this new and unfamiliar situation. Old habits inevitably take time to change, however. Frightening or unfamiliar feelings may be interpreted – by the person themselves or by relatives and helpers – as "symptoms" (possibly indicating imminent relapse) or even as totally inappropriate expressions of hostility.[169] *A common dilemma for many recovering people is that the range of behaviours and feelings that they are expected or allowed to display may have become extremely narrow.* In such cases, behaviours that challenge the "emotional status quo" may quickly give rise to conflicts, as the following example illustrates:

> The husband of a forty year old [woman with a diagnosis of schizophrenia] who was well stabilised on [neuroleptic medication] would suggest that she saw a doctor or get her medication changed at any show of irritability on her part, or whenever she expressed a wish to do something he did not want to. In general he seemed to see any change in her mood as being attributable to her illness, and possibly the beginnings of a relapse, rather than as an acceptable, normal variation. A result of this was that the [woman] tried to appear as placid as she could, particularly when she was with him. In other circles this would have been (and was) termed "blunting of affect".[172]

It often happens that a difficult – and perhaps painful – process of adjustment is called for by *everyone* concerned. For many people, learning how to handle and contain their feelings, and discovering ways of expressing them in a constructive, socially-acceptable manner, is a major task which must be dealt with if genuine progress is to occur. A real challenge for some people involves learning to accept that feelings of sadness, anxiety, uncertainty and many other painful emotions are just as much a part of being a whole human being as are the enjoyable feelings of happiness, pleasure and satisfaction. The tendency to "go numb", which many people experience whenever they are faced with *painful* feelings, can only be overcome as a person learns to accept, value and handle an ever-increasing range of emotions.

Letting Go

Anyone who has had low levels of motivation and energy over a long period of time may have come to rely on others to help and take care of them. If a person has also had significant problems with low self-esteem and a lack of self-confidence they may have even developed a tendency to *depend* on others to one degree or another. In some cases, family members who have been very supportive and protective may have become so used to giving care and assistance (often with very little in return) that it may have gradually become a way of life for them. Sometimes, a two-way state of *mutual* dependency may even have developed (this has been called "co-dependency"). For example, some relatives may have become so used to having a grown-up son or daughter relying on them that they might feel somewhat reluctant to see that person becoming more independent. Dr. Oliver Sacks encountered such a situation as some of his patients were beginning to improve:

> The restoration of activity and independence was by no means always welcomed by some of these relatives, and was sometimes passively or actively opposed. Some of these relatives had built their own lives around the illnesses of the patients, and – unconsciously, at least – did everything they could to reinforce the illness and dependence ensuing.[173]

As a previously dependent person begins to be more capable of taking care of themselves both they and others may need to make and accept significant changes to their habitual patterns of behaviour and ways of relating. Making such changes is often complicated by the fact that many people have mixed feelings about becoming more independent. Thus, the desire for more freedom and greater self-determination is often tempered by fear of the responsibilities that are necessarily involved. Though these issues can be very complex, the rewards of working through them soon become clear as every member of the family becomes empowered to grow beyond any limitations that their dependencies may have imposed.

Learning to Accept

When the best efforts of everyone have been made, and when everything that can humanly be done to improve a person's situation has been done, a time may come when it is necessary for all concerned to accept that – for the time being at least – it is not within anyone's power to bring about further progress. What this means, in short, is that some people may simply have to accept that, despite their desire to change, their capacity to do things may remain restricted. *The greatest challenge for some people may lie in learning to accept that many of their hopes and plans must be modified to fit in with the realities of their present abilities and circumstances.*

Despite whatever limitations circumstances may have imposed, *every* person always retains certain abilities which still make many things possible for them. It is vitally important that they try to do the most they can with these abilities. Rather than focusing on the opportunities that may have been lost, it is increasingly important at this stage for a person to focus on what opportunities still remain. A realistic – yet very hopeful – attitude to imposed limitations has been described by Patricia Deegan in the following way:

> Our recovery is marked by an ever-deepening acceptance of our limitations. But now, rather than being an occasion for despair, we find that our personal limitations are the ground from which spring our unique possibilities. This is the paradox of recovery, i.e. that in accepting what we cannot do or be, we begin to discover who we can be and what we can do.[174]

In the end, a person's ability to live a creative and satisfying life despite having some "negative" symptoms may depend to a large extent on their ability to develop just this kind of optimistic attitude. Many examples can be found of courageous people who have learned to live a full life within the limits that are imposed upon them by their circumstances. Many blind people learn to read Braille, for example, and, though their arms and legs are completely paralysed, some quadriplegic people even teach themselves to paint by holding brushes between their teeth. Such brave, extraordinary people have discovered that a change of heart may lead to a new way of life.

EPILOGUE:
THE DARK SIDE OF THE MOON

*Some Speculative Thoughts About "Negative" Symptoms
and Schizophrenia*

For many different reasons people often choose to "hide" what
they really think and feel. Some people, such as political
diplomats, judges, television news readers, and poker players *need*
to master the art of concealing their personal feelings whilst they
are in their professional roles. Common sense warns most people
not to reveal their deeper and more personal feelings and
thoughts unless they feel safe to do so. Consequently, a great deal
of what *anyone* is really experiencing may be kept well hidden
from others. By these ordinary, everyday acts of concealment a
socially acceptable "mask" is created and shown to the world. This
behaviour, so common that it may have even become necessary to
social survival, nevertheless involves a degree of "emotional shut-
down" and "self-protective withdrawal" which is taken for granted
by most people. In highly competitive Western societies it is often
only young children who are free to be spontaneously expressive
in the innocent way that many adults only dimly remember.

People who have a diagnosis of schizophrenia have many good
reasons for "hiding". One common reason is related to their fear
of being misunderstood or rejected. This fear may lead to one of
the most painful dilemmas experienced by anyone who has been
psychotic. In order to feel understood such a person needs to be
able to tell their personal story; to also feel accepted and
respected, however, they may need to conceal certain things that
others might not be able to understand (and may even judge or
mock). As a consequence, some experiences which may have
been personally meaningful and important – perhaps even some
"psychotic" experiences involving hallucinations or delusions –
may have to be kept hidden. Sometimes, the details of whole long
sections of a person's life (for example, time spent in hospital)
may never be comfortably shared with anyone, not even mental
health professionals. The long-term effect of this "closing up"
may be that a person learns to wear a "mask" behind which their
true feelings are forever hidden. In extreme cases, a person may

have become so used to "hiding" their real feelings that eventually even they themselves may no longer know what these feelings are!

We simply don't know how big a part these kinds of factors may play in contributing to "negative" symptoms. In some cases they may be very significant indeed. Jean Bouricius has given a graphic account of what can happen when a person doesn't feel able to reveal their true feelings. Her son, who had had a diagnosis of schizophrenia for 12 years, was considered to have "negative" symptoms because his face lacked expression, he had low energy, and he spoke infrequently. At the same time as he *appeared* to lack feelings, however, he was writing poetry which expressed very passionate emotions. This discrepancy between what was going on inside her son and what appeared on the outside, led his mother to ask:

> Is it possible that many persons who suffer from schizo-phrenia and exhibit negative symptoms are actually experiencing strong emotions that they are unable or afraid to express? I suspect that no observation of another person, especially one who is mentally ill, can disclose what is really going on in that person's mind. . . . The patient is an individual, and it is to be hoped that those who work with him will make every effort to find the emotions that may be hidden behind an expressionless face. I hope that all who have contact with a person suffering from schizophrenia will remember that [he] is experiencing not only the often frightening and painful things going on in his mind . . . but also the attitude of society toward him. Both these experiences might arouse emotions which could be overwhelming.[175]

Is this merely a misguided mother's plaintive plea? Very recent research has shown that even if they are expressing very little, people living with schizophrenia may still be experiencing emotions as intensely as other people do.[176] Whatever outward appearances may suggest, there is always a living person behind the "safety shield" created by aloofness and apathy. Sensitive observers have always known this. Professor Manfred Bleuler, for example, has found that even in the "worst chronic cases" – people who are sometimes described as being emotionally "burnt out" – there still exists a rich, active inner life and the capacity for experiencing fine emotions and human feelings. Professor Bleuler felt certain that even people who give the outward appearance of being totally withdrawn and unresponsive to the world around them still have the ability to feel, and are still capable of continuing to develop as a person.[177]

Whilst many powerful social pressures are tending to "push" a person into "closing up", other forces may be operating which exert a strong psychological "pull" on them from within. The psychiatrist Carl Jung, whose many brilliant insights into the psychology of schizophrenia[178] remain unequalled to this day, knew and described the true richness of the inner life of human beings. Jung believed that in the state referred to as schizophrenia it is sometimes as if a person's vital energy or "life force" had sunk back into its own depths, thereby leaving a mere shadow of the person that once was. This might happen for many reasons, but Jung felt it was far from being a hopeless situation because even when someone *appears* dull and apathetic, there may be more going on in their mind that is meaningful than there seems to be. Indeed, Jung was able to show that much of what occurs in "mental illness" is really only an exaggerated version – perhaps even a caricature – of what takes place to a lesser degree in *every* person as part of the vital human struggle toward wholeness.

Jung felt that the lack of engagement with the outer world so typical of people with "negative" symptoms resembles what occurs to every human being during the normal experience of dreaming. Whilst a person is dreaming their awareness is temporarily withdrawn from outer physical reality as it becomes increasingly absorbed into a private, inner world of imagination. In this way dreams allow every person to renew their connection with the mysteries of their inner world so that, refreshed and enriched, they will be ready once more to face the demands of life. The magical inner world of fantasy and imagination seems to exert a stronger "pull" over some people than does the outer world of everyday reality. The call of this private reality may even be almost irresistible at times, especially if ordinary life is empty and boring. The risk of getting stuck in this "wonderland" is also very real, however. If this does happen to someone, a period of extreme withdrawal, of being "shut in" by a low level of interest and a lack of energy for the outer world, may follow. Jung pointed out that, whilst such an experience can occur in a particularly intense way as part of schizophrenia, to one degree or another *everybody* may be susceptible to the lure of this kind of "psychological seduction":

> Anyone who observes himself, carefully and unsparingly, will know that there is something within him which would gladly hide and cover up all that is difficult and questionable in life, in order to smooth a path for itself. Insanity gives it a free hand. And once it has gained ascendancy, reality is veiled, more quickly or less; it becomes a distant dream, but the dream becomes a reality which holds the patient enchained, wholly or in part, often for the rest of his life. We healthy people, who stand with both feet in reality, see only the ruin of the patient in this world, but not the richness of that side of the psyche which is turned away from us. Unfortunately only too often no further knowledge reaches us of the things that are being played out on the dark side of the soul, because all the bridges have been broken down which connect that side with this.[179]

No one really knows what goes on in the apparently empty state of extreme withdrawal and emotional "shut-down". It seems probable that people go into this state for many different reasons and in response to many different needs. Sometimes, a period of intense inner absorption may even be a necessary prelude to a deep personal transformation. A person entering the "other world" who is eventually able to overcome its "pull" may emerge from their "psychological hibernation" stronger and wiser for the experience, and able to return to everyday life a more whole person than they were before. The fact that some people *do* eventually emerge from their "shut-down" state with a new feeling for living should encourage everyone to remain open to the possibility that, even in such an apparently "negative" situation, seeds of hope may still be sown. Patricia Deegan speaks from personal experience of this possibility:

> The truth is that at some point every single person who has been diagnosed with a mental illness passes through

> this time of anguish and giving up. Remember that giving up is a solution. We call it learning to play the game or learning to play dead. Giving up is a way of surviving in environments which are desolate, oppressive places and which fail to nurture and support us. . . . Thus, instead of seeing us as unmotivated, apathetic, or hopeless cases, we can be understood as people who are waiting. We never know for sure but perhaps, just perhaps, there is a new life within a person, just waiting to take root if a secure and nurturing soil is provided.[180]

It is increasingly common today for it to be said that people who receive a diagnosis of schizophrenia have only "broken brains" and incompetence, and that we all must wait – always patiently, often painfully – for the long-heralded "magic cure" that will fix the problem. But in this very attitude we risk losing the person more and more, a person who is already struggling to find and hold on to an acceptable sense of self. How will we understand and support them if we never even recognise the true nature of their lonely but very human struggle? And how will they even begin the task of rebuilding their life if they are told that their brain is incurably diseased? A very long time ago Carl Jung said something about schizophrenia that is well worth reflecting upon in our present "high-tech" era:

> Though we are still far from being able to explain all the relationships in that obscure world, we can maintain with complete assurance that in [schizophrenia] there is no symptom which could be described as psychologically groundless and meaningless. Even the most absurd things are nothing other than symbols for thoughts which are not only understandable in human terms but dwell in every human breast. In insanity we do not discover anything new and unknown; we are looking at the foundations of our own being, the matrix of those vital problems on which we are all engaged.[181]

Perhaps, when we are able to see that behind the glass wall of "negative" symptoms there is a suffering, afflicted, fighting and still living person, will we reach out with the wisdom and compassion that are the *true* medicines for the healing of the soul.

RECOMMENDED READING

Understanding and Helping the Schizophrenic by Silvano Arieti
(Penguin Books, 1981)
A highly recommended and practical book which provides a simple and clear description of the inner world and experiences of people who have a diagnosis of schizophrenia. Professor Arieti emphasises the difficult emotional conflicts which often precede the onset of psychosis and how they can contribute to the development of symptoms, both "positive" and "negative".

The Dinosaur Man: Tales of Madness and Enchantment from the Back Ward by Susan Baur
(New York: HarperPerennial, 1992)
This book was written by a clinical psychologist who set out to describe the years she spent working with hospitalised, "chronic" psychiatric patients. Her very touching stories reveal the many extraordinary ways these terribly isolated human beings find to create a sense of meaning in their lives. She movingly describes how communication became possible as she gradually learnt to allow herself to remain open to the unexpected.

Memories, Dreams, Reflections by C. G. Jung
(London: Fontana, 1983)
Written at the end of his long and extremely productive life, this book is Jung's autobiography. It contains a graphic description of his own encounter with psychosis and subsequent recovery. It is an excellent introduction to many of the pioneering ideas that make Jung a true "healer of the soul".

Echoes of the Early Tides: A Healing Journey by Tony Moore
(Sydney: HarperCollins, 1994)
With great sensitivity and compassion, the author of this book (who also wrote the best-selling "Cry of the Damaged Man") describes how even in the depths of sorrow hope persists for the life still waiting to be touched. Especially recommended for those whose losses have led to feelings of reduced self-worth. A celebration of the uniqueness and sacredness of all individuals.

Awakenings by Oliver Sacks
(London: Picador, 1991)
In this remarkable account of the lives of the last survivors of the

great sleeping-sickness epidemic of the 1920s, the renowned neurologist Oliver Sacks describes the "awakening" of patients, some of whom had spent decades in utter isolation. A profound testimony to the tenacity of the human spirit which explores in a sensitive, thought-provoking way questions regarding health, disease, suffering, care and the human condition. An extraordinary story told by a unique healer.

Peace, Love and Healing: Bodymind Communication and the Path to Self-Healing by Bernie Siegel
(New York: Harper and Row, 1989)
Dr. Siegel, a physician and surgeon, is one of the leading practitioners and teachers of holistic health care in the world today. In this wonderful book he discusses the importance of self-healing, and the physiological effects of love, joy and optimism. Very highly recommended to anyone interested in the connections between healing, wholeness, and spirituality.

Hearing Voices: A Self-Help Guide and Reference Book
by John Watkins
(Melbourne, Victoria: Richmond Fellowship of Victoria, 1993)
This small book provides a wealth of information about the experience of hearing voices which will help to reduce fear and promote understanding of this surprisingly common experience. A wide range of practical coping strategies are described which many people may find helpful in their attempts to deal with voices that are distressing.

The Seduction of Madness: Revolutionary Insights into the World of Psychosis and a Compassionate Approach to Recovery at Home by Edward Podvoll
(New York: HarperCollins, 1990)
Edward Podvoll is a psychiatrist who has spent many years studying the psychotic state and the processes of recovery. In this book Dr. Podvoll describes in great detail his unique understanding of what psychosis is and why it occurs. Of particular importance is his discovery of ways to recognise and work with the ever-present potential for true sanity which exists even within the psychotic mind, and which provides the ultimate basis from which recovery eventually grows.

When The Spirits Come Back by Janet Dallett
(Toronto: Inner City Books, 1988)
Written by a Jungian therapist, this book is a touching account of
one woman's personal struggle to find ways to serve life and soul
whilst fulfilling her responsibilities as a mental health professional. The author's thought-provoking views on psychosis are
grounded in her belief that a respectful attitude toward the
deepest spiritual levels of the psyche is crucial to true emotional
healing.

Recovering Our Sense of Value After Being Labelled Mentally Ill by
Patricia Deegan
(*Journal of Psychosocial Nursing*, Vol.31, No.4, 1993)
Patricia Deegan is a former psychiatric patient who is now a
leading spokesperson in the consumer movement. In this article
she provides a heart-rending account of the process of "spirit
breaking" as it is experienced by many people who have under-
gone psychosis and its psychological and social aftermath. Her
message of healing and recovery provides an example and a
powerful source of inspiration to all who have suffered through
their own "dark night of the soul".

Recovery From Schizophrenia: A Personal Odyssey
by Marcia Lovejoy
(*Hospital and Community Psychiatry*, Vol.35, No.8, 1984)
Marcia Lovejoy explains in this article why hope is an essential
element in the recovery process. She describes how her own
recovery from schizophrenia was helped by a combination of
treatment approaches, including some non-traditional ones. She
explains how taking responsibility for herself and learning to use
practical coping strategies eventually led her from despair and
suffering to hope and recovery.

Healing and Wholeness by John Sanford
(New York: Paulist Press, 1977)
This is a book for anyone interested in finding ways to bring more
health and wholeness into their life. The author attempts to show
where healing comes from and how a person can learn to tap into
the healing potential which exists within. The book provides a
clear and simple explanation of some of the basic principles of
Carl Jung's psychology and an excellent summary of his views on
the nature of psychosis.

NOTES

1 Sacks, 1986, p.4.
2 Strauss et al., 1989, p.128.
3 DSM-IV, American Psychiatric Association, 1994
4 Torrey, 1988.
5 Strauss, 1985.
6 Strauss et al., 1989, p.128.
7 DSM-IV, American Psychiatric Association, 1994, p.277.
8 Zubin and Steinhauer, 1981, p.479.
9 Kaplan and Sadock, 1981, p.310.
10 Kaplan and Sadock, 1981.
11 Cited in Hatfield and Lefley, 1993, p.119.
12 Bleuler, 1950, p.65.
13 Arieti, 1981, p.165.
14 Carpenter et al., 1985, p.443.
15 Wing, 1978.
16 Abrahamson, 1993.
17 Carpenter et al., 1985, p.443.
18 Wing, 1978.
19 Strauss, 1989a, p.184, emphasis added.
20 Ruocchio, 1991, p.359.
21 Bleuler, 1950, p.460, emphasis added.
22 Tantam, 1983.
23 Eigen, 1993, p.101.
24 Frankl, 1963, p.35.
25 Hayward and Taylor, 1956, p.236.
26 Unzicker, 1989, p.71.
27 McGlashan, 1982.
28 Cited in Chapman, 1966, p.231.
29 Carr, 1983.
30 Benjamin, 1989; Watkins, 1993.
31 Farr, 1982, p.3.
32 Minas et al., 1988.
33 Falloon, 1987, p.181.
34 DSM-IV, American Psychiatric Association, 1994.
35 DSM-IV, American Psychiatric Association, 1994, p.425.
36 Shaner and Eth, 1989.
37 McGorry et al., 1991.
38 Stampfer, 1990.
39 Deegan, 1993, p.10.
40 McGlashan and Carpenter, 1976.
41 Strauss, 1989b, p.24.
42 Kayton et al., 1976.
43 Vonnegut, 1976, p. 251.
44 Hatfield and Lefley, 1993.
45 Carpenter et al., 1985, p.447.
46 Strauss et al., 1989.
47 Moore, 1991, p.86.
48 Deegan, 1988, p.13.
49 Strauss, 1985.
50 Selzer et al., 1989, p.57.
51 Zubin, 1985, p.466.
52 Cited in Hatfield and Lefley, 1993, p.127.
53 Strauss et al., 1989, p.131.
54 Deegan, 1992a, p.12.
55 Cited in Rollin, 1980, p.125.
56 Lovejoy, 1982, p.606.
57 Deegan, 1993, p.8.
58 Deegan, 1989, p.6.
59 McGlashan and Carpenter, 1976.
60 Van Putten and May, 1978; Becker, 1988.
61 Carpenter et al., 1985; DSM-IV, American Psychiatric Association, 1994.
62 Corin and Lauzon, 1992.
63 Arieti, 1981, p.90.
64 Guntrip, 1962.

65 Venables and Wing, 1962.
66 A Recovering Patient, 1986, p.68.
67 Hatfield and Lefley, 1993.
68 Wing, 1978.
69 Halford et al., 1991.
70 Wing, 1978, p.606.
71 DSM-IV, American Psychiatric Association, 1994, p.277.
72 Tantam, 1983.
73 Healy, 1993.
74 Bleuler, 1986, p.8
75 Ciompi, 1994.
76 Healy, 1989.
77 Ayd, 1973, p.372.
78 Rifkin et al., 1978; Torrey, 1988.
79 Kaplan and Sadock, 1981, p.784.
80 Wescott, 1979, p.989.
81 Wallace, 1994.
82 Bockes, 1985, p.488.
83 Carpenter et al., 1985.
84 Blaska, 1990.
85 Torrey, 1988.
86 Leach, 1991.
87 Birchwood et al., 1989, p.86.
88 Torrey, 1988, p.133.
89 Ciompi, 1988.
90 Crow, 1983, p.81.
91 Sacks, 1991, p.21.
92 Strauss et al., 1989.
93 Ciompi, 1989; Gabbard, 1992.
94 Weinberger, 1984.
95 Bleuler, 1978; Ciompi, 1980; Barham and Hayward, 1990.
96 Strauss et al., 1989.
97 Farr, 1982, p.7, emphasis added.
98 Wing, 1978.
99 Cited in Rollin, 1980, p.125.
100 Podvoll, 1990, p.295.
101 Ludwig, 1971.
102 Ciompi, 1980.

103 DSM-IV, American Psychiatric Association, 1994.
104 Selzer et al., 1989, p.13.
105 Strauss et al., 1989.
106 Wing, 1978.
107 Goldman and Quinn, 1988.
108 Halford et al., 1991.
109 Glass et al., 1989.
110 Harding et al., 1987.
111 Bleuler, 1968, p.6.
112 Bleuler, 1974, p.247.
113 Cited in Barham and Hayward, 1990, p.68.
114 Ciompi, 1988.
115 DSM-IV, American Psychiatric Association, 1994.
116 Carpenter et al., 1988.
117 Lovejoy, 1982.
118 Deegan, 1988, p.14.
119 Ciompi, 1983, p.62.
120 Bleuler, 1986, p.8.
121 Bleuler, 1978.
122 Hayward and Taylor, 1956, p.212.
123 Halford et al., 1991.
124 Leete, 1993.
125 Leete, 1993, p.124.
126 Leete, 1993, p.125.
127 Creer, 1978, p.236.
128 Torrey, 1988.
129 Tantam, 1983.
130 Bleuler, 1978.
131 Gardos and Cole, 1976.
132 Carpenter et al., 1985.
133 Ayd, 1973; Torrey, 1988.
134 Torrey, 1988; Bitter et al., 1991.
135 Herz et al., 1989.
136 Torrey, 1988.
137 Dallett, 1988, p.15.
138 Pierce, 1987, p.93.
139 Pierce, 1988, p.147.
140 Hatfield, 1989, p1143.
141 Beavis, 1992, p.23.
142 Bleuler, 1978.

143   Cited in Rosenbaum, 1970, p.81.
144   Goff et al., 1992.
145   Glass et al., 1989.
146   A Recovering Patient, 1986, pp.69-70.
147   Bouricius, 1989.
148   Falloon, 1987; Carr, 1988.
149   Watkins, 1993.
150   Rollin, 1980.
151   Cited in Rollin, 1980, p.126.
152   Carpenter et al., 1985.
153   Gallo, 1994, p.410.
154   Siegel, 1989, p.220.
155   Bleuler, 1978.
156   Carpenter et al., 1985.
157   Van Putten and May, 1978; Johnson, 1984.
158   Becker, 1988.
159   Van Putten and May, 1978, p.1106.
160   Becker, 1988.

161   Watkins, 1993.
162   Podvoll, 1990.
163   Boisen, 1971; Podvoll, 1990.
164   Deegan, 1988, p.13
165   Ingerman, 1991.
166   Sullivan, 1993.
167   Deegan, 1993, pp.9-11.
168   Ruocchio, 1989, p.165.
169   Mason et al., 1990.
170   Deegan, 1993, p.8.
171   Podvoll, 1990.
172   Atkinson, 1986, p.92.
173   Sacks, 1991, p.213.
174   Deegan, 1988, p.14.
175   Bouricius, 1989, p.207.
176   Kring et al., 1993.
177   Bleuler, 1978.
178   Jung, 1974.
179   Jung, 1982, p.177.
180   Deegan, 1992b, p.8.3.
181   Jung, 1982, p.178.

REFERENCES

A Recovering Patient (1986) "Can We Talk?" The Schizophrenic Patient in Psychotherapy. *American Journal of Psychiatry*, Vol.143.

Abrahamson, D. (1993) Institutionalisation and the Long-Term Course of Schizophrenia. *British Journal of Psychiatry*, Vol.162.

American Psychiatric Association (1994) *Diagnostic and Statistical Manual of Mental Disorders – Fourth Edition (DSM-IV)*. Washington, DC: American Psychiatric Association.

Arieti, S. (1981) *Understanding and Helping the Schizophrenic: A Guide for Family and Friends*. Harmondsworth: Penguin Books.

Atkinson, J. (1986) *Schizophrenia at Home*. London: Croom Helm.

Ayd, F. (1973) Rational Pharmacotherapy: Once-A-Day Drug Dosage. *Diseases of the Nervous System*, Vol.34.

Barham, P. and Hayward, R. (1990) Schizophrenia As A Life Process. In: Bentall, R. (ed.) *Reconstructing Schizophrenia*. London: Routledge.

Beavis, J. (1992) Psychosis and Spirituality. *Word Salad*, December, 1992.

Benjamin, L. (1989) Is Chronicity a Function of the Relationship between the Person and the Auditory Hallucination? *Schizophrenia Bulletin*, Vol.15, No.2.

Becker, R. (1988) Depression in Schizophrenia. *Hospital and Community Psychiatry*, Vol.39, No.12.

Birchwood, M., Hallett, S. and Preston, M. (1989) *Schizophrenia: An Integrated Approach to Research and Treatment*. New York: New York University Press.

Bitter, I., Volavka, J. and Scheurer, J. (1991) The Concept of the Neuroleptic Threshold: An Update. *Journal of Clinical Psychopharmacology*, Vol.11, No.1.

Blaska, B. (1990) The Myriad Medication Mistakes in Psychiatry: A Consumer's View. *Hospital and Community Psychiatry*, Vol.41, No.9.

Bleuler, E. (1950) *Dementia Praecox or The Group of Schizophrenias*. New York: International Universities Press.

Bleuler, M. (1968) A 23-Year Longitudinal Study of 208 Schizophrenics and Impressions in Regard to the Nature of Schizophrenia. In: Rosenthal, D. and Kety, S. (eds.) *The Transmission of Schizophrenia*. New York: Pergamon Press.

Bleuler, M. (1974) The Long-Term Course of the Schizophrenic Psychoses. *Psychological Medicine*, Vol.4.

Bleuler, M. (1978) *The Schizophrenic Disorders. Long-Term Patient and Family Studies*. New Haven: Yale University Press.

Bleuler, M. (1986) Introduction and Overview. In: Burrows, G., Norman, T., and Rubinstein, G. (eds.) *Handbook of Studies on Schizophrenia.* Amsterdam: Elsevier.

Bockes, Z. (1985) First Person Account: "Freedom" Means Knowing You Have A Choice. *Schizophrenia Bulletin.* Vol.11, No.3.

Boisen, A. (1971) *The Exploration of the Inner World: A Study of Mental Disorder and Religious Experience.* Philadelphia: University of Philadelphia Press.

Bouricius, J. (1989) Negative Symptoms and Emotions in Schizophrenia. *Schizophrenia Bulletin,* Vol.15, No.2.

Carpenter, W., Heinrichs, D., and Alphs, L. (1985) Treatment of Negative Symptoms. *Schizophrenia Bulletin,* Vol.11, No.3.

Carpenter, W., Heinrichs, D. and Wagman, A. (1988) Deficit and Nondeficit Forms of Schizophrenia: The Concept. *American Journal Of Psychiatry,* Vol.145.

Carr, V. (1983) Recovery From Schizophrenia: A Review of Patterns of Psychosis. *Schizophrenia Bulletin,* Vol.9, No.1.

Carr, V. (1988) Patient's Techniques for Coping with Schizophrenia: An Exploratory Study. *British Journal of Medical Psychology,* Vol.61.

Chapman, J. (1966) The Early Symptoms of Schizophrenia. *British Journal of Psychiatry,* Vol.112.

Ciompi, L. (1980) The Natural History of Schizophrenia In the Long Term. *British Journal of Psychiatry,* Vol.136.

Ciompi, L. (1983) How to Improve the Treatment of Schizophrenics: A Multicausal Illness Concept and Its Therapeutic Consequences. In: Stierlin, H., Wynne, L. and Wirsching, M. (eds.) *Psychosocial Intervention in Schizophrenia: An International View.* Berlin: Springer-Verlag.

Ciompi, L. (1988) Learning From Outcome Studies. Toward A Comprehensive Biological-Psychosocial Understanding of Schizophrenia. *Schizophrenia Research,* Vol.1.

Ciompi, L. (1989) The Dynamics of Complex Biological-Psychosocial Systems. Four Fundamental Psycho-Biological Mediators in the Long-Term Evolution of Schizophrenia. *British Journal of Psychiatry,* Vol.155 (suppl.5).

Ciompi, L. (1994) Affect Logic: An Integrative Model of the Psyche and its Relations to Schizophrenia. *British Journal of Psychiatry,* Vol.164 (suppl.23).

Corin, E. and Lauzon, G. (1992) Positive Withdrawal and the Quest for Meaning: The Reconstruction of Experience among Schizophrenics. *Psychiatry,* Vol.55.

Creer, C. (1978) Social Work with Patients and their Families. In: Wing, J. (ed.) *Schizophrenia: Towards a New Synthesis.* London: Academic Press.

Crow, T. (1983) Schizophrenic Deterioration (Discussion). *British Journal of Psychiatry,* Vol.143.

Dallett, J. (1988) *When The Spirits Come Back.* Toronto: Inner City Books.

Deegan, P. (1988) Recovery: The Lived Experience of Rehabilitation. *Psychosocial Rehabilitation Journal,* Vol.11, No.4.

Deegan, P. (1989) A Letter To My Friend Who Is Giving Up. *Keynote Address: Connecticut Conference on Supported Employment,* Cromwell, Connecticut.

Deegan, P. (1992a) The Independent Living Movement and People with Psychiatric Disabilities: Taking Back Control Over Our Own Lives. *Psychosocial Rehabilitation Journal,* Vol.15, No.3.

Deegan, P. (1992b) Recovery, Rehabilitation and the Conspiracy of Hope. *Keynote Address: Western Regional Conference on Housing and Supports,* Portland, Oregon.

Deegan, P. (1993) Recovering Our Sense of Value After Being Labelled Mentally Ill. *Journal of Psychosocial Nursing,* Vol.31, No.4.

Eigen, M. (1993) *The Psychotic Core.* New Jersey: Jason Aronson.

Falloon, I. (1987) Cognitive and Behavioural Interventions in the Self Control of Schizophrenia. In: Strauss, J. et al. (eds.) *Psychosocial Treatment of Schizophrenia.* New York: Hans Huber.

Farr, E. (1982) A Personal Account of Schizophrenia. In: Tsuang, M. *Schizophrenia: The Facts.* Oxford: Oxford University Press.

Frankl, V. (1963) *Man's Search For Meaning: An Introduction to Logotherapy.* New York: Pocket Books.

Gabbard, G. (1992) Psychodynamic Psychiatry in the "Decade of the Brain". *American Journal of Psychiatry,* Vol.149, No.8.

Gallo, K. (1994) First Person Account: Self-Stigmatization. *Schizophrenia Bulletin,* Vol.20, No.2.

Gardos, G. and Cole, J. (1976) Maintenance Antipsychotic Therapy: Is the Cure Worse than the Disease? *American Journal of Psychiatry,* Vol.133, No.1.

Glass, L., Katz, H., Schnitzer, R., Knapp, P., Frank, A., and Gunderson, J. (1989) Psychotherapy of Schizophrenia: An Empirical Investigation of the Relationship of Process to Outcome. *American Journal of Psychiatry,* Vol.146, No.5.

Goff, D., Henderson, D. and Amico, E. (1992) Cigarette Smoking in Schizophrenia: Relationship to Psychopathology and Medication Side Effects. *American Journal of Psychiatry,* Vol.149, No.9.

Goldman, C. and Quinn, F. (1988) Effects of a Patient Education Program in the Treatment of Schizophrenia. *Hospital and Community Psychiatry,* Vol.39, No.3.

Guntrip, H. (1962) The Schizoid Compromise and Psychotherapeutic Stalemate. *British Journal of Medical Psychology,* Vol.35.

Halford, W., Schweitzer, R. and Varghese, F. (1991) Effects of Family Environment on Negative Symptoms and Quality of Life of Psychotic Patients. *Hospital and Community Psychiatry,* Vol.42, No.12.

Harding, C., Zubin, J. and Strauss, J. (1987) Chronicity in Schizophrenia: Fact, Partial Fact, or Artefact? *Hospital and Community Psychiatry,* Vol.38, No.5.

Hatfield, A. (1989) Patients' Accounts of Stress and Coping in Schizophrenia. *Hospital and Community Psychiatry,* Vol.40, No.11.

Hatfield, A. and Lefley, H. (1993) *Surviving Mental Illness.* New York: The Guildford Press.

Hayward, M. and Taylor, J. (1956) A Schizophrenic Patient Describes the Action of Intensive Psychotherapy. *Psychiatric Quarterly,* Vol.30.

Healy, D. (1989) Neuroleptics and Psychic Indifference: A Review. *Journal of the Royal Society of Medicine,* Vol.82.

Healy, D. (1993) *Psychiatric Drugs Explained.* London: Mosby.

Herz, M., Glazer, W., Mirza, M., Mostert, M. and Hafez, H. (1989) Treating Prodromal Episodes to Prevent Relapse in Schizophrenia. *British Journal of Psychiatry,* Vol.155 (suppl.5).

Ingerman, S. (1991) *Soul Retrieval: Mending the Fragmented Self.* New York: HarperCollins.

Johnson, D. (1984) Observations on the Use of Long-Acting Depot Neuroleptic Injections in the Maintenance Therapy of Schizophrenia. *Journal Of Clinical Psychiatry,* Vol.45, No.5, Sec.2.

Jung, C.G. (1974) *The Psychology of Dementia Praecox.* Princeton, Princeton University Press.

Jung, C.G. (1982) *The Psychogenesis of Mental Disease.* Princeton: Princeton University Press.

Kaplan, H. and Sadock, B. (1981) *Modern Synopsis of Comprehensive Textbook of Psychiatry/III (Third Edition).* Baltimore: Williams and Wilkins.

Kayton, L., Beck, J. and Koh, S. (1976) Postpsychotic State, Convalescent Environment, and Therapeutic Relationship in Schizophrenic Outcome. *American Journal of Psychiatry,* Vol.133, No.11.

Kring, A., Kerr, S., Smith, D., and Neale, J. (1993) Flat Affect Does Not Reflect Diminished Subjective Experience of Emotion. *Journal of Abnormal Psychology,* Vol.102, No.4.

Leach, A. (1991) Negative Symptoms. *Current Opinion in Psychiatry,* Vol.4.

Leete, E. (1993) The Interpersonal Environment: A Consumer's Personal Recollection. In: Hatfield, A. and Lefley, H. *Surviving Mental Illness.* New York: The Guildford Press.

Lovejoy, M. (1982) Expectations and the Recovery Process. *Schizophrenia Bulletin,* Vol.8, No.4.

Ludwig, A. (1971) *Treating the Treatment Failures: The Challenge of Chronic Schizophrenia.* New York: Grune and Stratton.

Mason, S., Gingerich, S. and Siris, S. (1990) Patients' and Caregivers' Adaptation to Improvements in Schizophrenia. *Hospital and Community Psychiatry,* Vol.41, No.5.

McGlashan, T. (1982) Aphanisis: The Syndrome of Pseudo-Depression in Chronic Schizophrenia. *Schizophrenia Bulletin*, Vol.8, No.1.

McGlashan, T. and Carpenter, W. (1976) Postpsychotic Depression in Schizophrenia. *Archives of General Psychiatry*, Vol.33.

McGorry, P., Chanen, A., McCarthy, E., Van Riel, R., McKenzie, D. and Singh, B. (1991) Posttraumatic Stress Disorder Following Recent-Onset Psychosis. *Journal of Nervous and Mental Disease*, Vol.179, No.5.

Minas, I., Joshua, S., Jackson, H. and Burgess, P. (1988) Persistent Psychotic Symptoms at Discharge in Patients with Schizophrenia. *Australian and New Zealand Journal of Psychiatry*, Vol.22.

Moore, T. (1991) *Cry of the Damaged Man. A Personal Journey of Recovery.* Sydney: Pan Macmillan.

Pierce, E. (1987) *Ordinary Insanity.* P.E.Pierce: Dulwich Hill, NSW, Australia.

Pierce, E. (1988) *Passion for the Possible.* P.E.Pierce: Gladesville, NSW, Australia.

Podvoll, E. (1990) *The Seduction of Madness.* New York: HarperCollins.

Rifkin, A., Quitkin, F. and Klein, D. (1975) Akinesia: A Poorly Recognised Drug-Induced Extrapyramidal Behavioral Disorder. *Archives of General Psychiatry*, Vol.32.

Rollin, H. (ed.) (1980) *Coping With Schizophrenia.* London: National Schizophrenia Fellowship of Britain.

Rosenbaum, C. (1970) *The Meaning of Madness.* New York: Science House.

Ruocchio, P. (1989) First Person Account: Fighting the Fight – The Schizophrenic's Nightmare. *Schizophrenia Bulletin*, Vol.15, No.1.

Ruocchio, P. (1991) First Person Account: The Schizophrenic Inside. *Schizophrenia Bulletin*, Vol.17, No.2.

Sacks, O. (1986) *The Man Who Mistook His Wife for a Hat.* London: Picador.

Sacks, O. (1991) *Awakenings.* London: Picador.

Selzer, M., Sullivan, T., Carsky, M. and Terkelsen, K. (1989) *Working with the Person with Schizophrenia.* New York: New York University Press.

Shaner, A. and Eth, S. (1989) *Can Schizophrenia Cause Posttraumatic Stress Disorder?* American Journal of Psychotherapy, Vol.XLIII, No.4.

Siegel, B. (1989) *Peace, Love and Healing.* New York: Harper and Row.

Stampfer, H. (1990) "Negative Symptoms": A Cumulative Trauma Stress Disorder? *Australian and New Zealand Journal of Psychiatry*, Vol.24.

Strauss, J. (1985) Negative Symptoms: Future Developments of the Concept. *Schizophrenia Bulletin*, Vol.11, No.3.

Strauss, J. (1989a) Subjective Experiences of Schizophrenia: Toward a New Dynamic Psychiatry – II. *Schizophrenia Bulletin*, Vol.15, No.2.

Strauss, J. (1989b) Mediating Processes in Schizophrenia: Towards a New Dynamic Psychiatry. *British Journal of Psychiatry*, Vol.155 (suppl.5).

Strauss, J., Rakfeldt, J., Harding, C. and Lieberman, P. (1989) Psychological and Social Aspects of Negative Symptoms. *British Journal of Psychiatry,* Vol.155 (suppl.7).

Sullivan, W. (1993) "It Helps Me Be A Whole Person": The Role of Spirituality Among the Mentally Challenged. *Psychosocial Rehabilitation Journal,* Vol.16, No.3.

Tantam, D. (1983) Schizophrenic Deterioration (Discussion). *British Journal of Psychiatry,* Vol.143.

Torrey, E. (1988) *Surviving Schizophrenia: A Family Manual (Revised Edition).* New York: Harper and Row.

Unzicker, R. (1989) On My Own: A Personal Journey Through Madness and Re-Emergence. *Psychosocial Rehabilitation Journal,* Vol.13, No.1.

Van Putten, T. and May, P. (1978) "Akinetic Depression" in Schizophrenia. *Archives of General Psychiatry,* Vol.35.

Venables, P. and Wing, J. (1962) Level of Arousal and Subclassification of Schizophrenia. *Archives of General Psychiatry,* Vol.7.

Vonnegut, M. (1976) *The Eden Express.* New York: Bantam.

Wallace, M. (1994) Schizophrenia – A National Emergency: Preliminary Observations on SANELINE. *Acta Psychiatrica Scandinavica,* Vol.89, (suppl.380).

Watkins, J. (1993) *Hearing Voices: A Self-Help Guide and Reference Book.* Melbourne: Richmond Fellowship of Victoria.

Weinberger, D. (1984) Computed Tomography Findings in Schizophrenia: Speculation on the Meaning of It All. *Journal of Psychiatric Research,* Vol.18.

Wescott, P. (1979) One Man's Schizophrenic Illness. *British Medical Journal,* Vol.1.

Wing, J. (1978) Social Influences on the Course of Schizophrenia. In: Wynne, L., Cromwell, R. and Matthysse, S. (eds.) *The Nature of Schizophrenia: New Approaches to Research and Treatment.* New York: John Wiley and Sons.

Zubin, J. (1985) Negative Symptoms: Are They Indigenous to Schizophrenia? *Schizophrenia Bulletin,* Vol.11, No.3.

Zubin, J. and Steinhauer, S. (1981) How to Break the Logjam in Schizophrenia. *Journal of Nervous and Mental Disease,* Vol.169, No.8.

INDEX